THE BROWN GORAS OF BRAMPTON

Struggles in a Land of Promise

THE BROWN GORAS OF BRAMPTON

Struggles in a Land of Promise

Aparjeet Nakai

THE BROWSER
Publishers and Booksellers

The Brown Goras of Brampton:
Struggles in a Land of Promise
by Aparjeet Nakai

ISBN: 978-93-92210-40-2
Imprint: The Browser

Published by:
JGS Enterprises Pvt Ltd
SCO 14-15, Sector 8-C,
Chandigarh 160 009
Website – thebrowser.org
Email – service@thebrowser.in

Printed in India

Cover Design © 99beagles.com

THE BROWSER
Publishers and Booksellers

For those who choose love over prejudice, this is dedicated to you

Contents

Prologue

As I strolled through Coronation Park near the Toronto waterfront on a crisp Canadian afternoon, I couldn't help but notice a young man seated on a bench, his face etched with a mixture of hope and despair. We had shared smiles earlier, recognizing each other as part of the same community because we both wore turbans. Approaching him, I offered a friendly smile again and started a conversation.

'How are you faring here?' I inquired, genuinely curious about his experiences in this new land.

The young man, his eyes reflecting a tumultuous journey, sighed deeply before responding, 'Life has been difficult, but back in India, I wouldn't have escaped the near-poverty conditions that held me tightly there.'

Intrigued, I pressed further, 'What has been the most challenging part of your journey here?'

He hesitated for a moment, then said, 'Finding work to meet my living expenses. My dad finds it increasingly difficult to send me money to support me.'

Sympathy welled up inside me, knowing the immense pressure that economic hardships could bring. 'I'm sorry to hear that,' I offered, wondering if there was more to his story.

As if sensing my unspoken question, he continued, 'You know, it's not just the financial struggles. It's also about the discrimination we face.'

'Discrimination?' I raised an eyebrow, puzzled.

'You mean racism?'

He shook his head, 'No, not from the whites. I don't face racism from them. It's the senior members of my community, those who moved here between the 1970s and 1990s, that make life tough for newcomers like me.'

I leaned in, eager to understand his perspective. 'Why do they discriminate against you?'

With a heavy sigh, he replied, 'They're our nemesis. They treat us newcomers as second-class citizens. They overcharge for overcrowded basement accommodations and ill-treat us.'

My heart sank, imagining the hardship he must endure. 'I had no idea,' I admitted.

He wasn't finished, his voice tinged with frustration. 'Have you seen or heard what the Punjabi media in Canada put out?'

I shook my head, confessing my ignorance.

'Well,' he continued, 'you need to. It's toxic towards the Punjabi immigrants coming in now. Anyone who's been here for five to seven years thinks they have the right to be disrespectful towards us, denouncing us as a problem rather than appreciating our struggles and supporting us.'

His revelations took me aback. This young man's story was shedding light on an aspect of the immigrant experience I had never considered. The unity that I had assumed must exist among members of the same community appeared shattered, replaced by the painful reality of discrimination and division.

As we sat there, the young man shared more of his experiences, speaking of the challenges of finding a job in his field despite being highly educated and skilled. He recounted stories of social gatherings where he felt like an outsider, unwelcome among his own people who had settled there decades earlier.

Listening to him, I couldn't help but feel a growing sense of unease. The promise of a better life in Canada, a land known for its diversity and inclusivity, seemed tarnished in his eyes. He longed for acceptance and support but often found judgment and prejudice instead. Our conversation continued, and as the sun dipped below the horizon, I couldn't help but reflect on the complexities of immigration. It was a journey filled with hope and hardship, unity and division, and dreams realized and shattered.

As I walked back home from that encounter with the young man, his words weighed heavily on my mind. I could not shake the feeling that his experiences might not be unique. Was he just one individual grappling with a tough situation, or were there others like him facing similar challenges in this land of promise? Determined to find the answers, I decided to embark on a journey of discovery.

Introduction

The title of this book could well be about Southall or Hounslow in the UK, or Blacktown in Sydney, or even Surrey in British Columbia in Canada. While most individuals I interviewed for this book were from Brampton and Mississauga, Ontario, I observed similar undercurrents when engaging with Indian communities in the UK, Australia, and New Zealand.

Three things motivated me to write this book.

First, during my recent visit to Canada in May 2023, I found myself increasingly concerned about the state of immigrant communities, particularly the Punjabi diaspora, and the division that seemed to be growing within these communities. During this time, I listened to the Punjabi media in Canada, and it left me deeply disturbed, as it appeared biased against new immigrants, portraying them in a negative light by exaggerating accounts of crimes committed by them. It seemed as if everything wrong in Canada was attributable to them. The talk shows on these channels often featured self-proclaimed experts who, in my opinion, did not possess the necessary education or understanding to provide a fair and balanced perspective.

The second reason was a chance encounter at a housewarming party and religious function in Mississauga. I met there an elderly individual whose beliefs and animosity towards international students from India were particularly toxic and unreasonable. He left an indelible mark on me, catalyzing me to explore the depths of hatred and to understand and address it.

The third and most significant reason was my interactions with students and young immigrants from India, predominantly of Punjabi and Gujarati origins. Even though my two daughters are part of this group, I exclude them as I consider them more privileged than most other students because they had already traveled the world, visiting many countries on solo trips, and did not step into Canada as dependent on relatives who may have viewed them as a threat or a financial burden. Fortunately, my finances allowed me to keep them away from the infamous 'Indian aunties'. Nevertheless, that did not stop me from empathizing with other younger newcomers. The dialogues I had with these individuals enriched me, allowing me to understand the psychology of hatred they faced and how it can be countered to elevate one's self-esteem.

I share with the reader the underlying reasons for the divide within the Indian community in Canada and suggest remedies to mitigate it. While I focus on the Punjabi community due to my background, similar dynamics exist within other Indian, Asian, and African communities. Regardless of your ethnicity, I urge you to read on, as you may find parallels to your community here.

This book is not only a reflection on Canada but a mirror to immigrant communities worldwide in the twenty-first century. While my exploration is grounded in the Canadian context, similar narratives exist in countries such as the UK, the US, and Australia. Consider this a case study that can undoubtedly apply to other countries experiencing immigration.

As we delve into the heart of immigrant communities, I hope this book serves as a bridge, connecting individuals from different backgrounds, fostering empathy, and encouraging dialogue. I sincerely hope that more Canadians will read this book to gain insight into the intricacies of immigration and the stories that unfold. Through understanding, we can work together to build a more inclusive and harmonious society.

All the encounters mentioned in the book are based on actual events. To protect the anonymity of the individuals involved, I have altered or omitted their names. The only exceptions are the artists Sandeep Johal and Manjit Singh Chatrik of Vancouver and Montreal, respectively, whose real names I have used.

Together, we can work towards bridging divides and creating a more compassionate and interconnected world.

Parleys on the GO

On a recent ride on a GO train[1] from Union Station to Brampton, I realized that the daily commuters held the key to unraveling this complex issue. I needed to engage with the young Indian individuals heading to work, studies, and back. However, I knew it wouldn't be easy to get them to open up. They might assume I was one of the earlier settlers, as my age would indicate.

To navigate this delicate task, I would have to make it clear from the start that I was not an older immigrant but a visitor there to see my daughter. I would also have to pretend that I didn't have relatives and friends in Canada. Armed with these pretexts, I decided to venture onto the train, eager to connect with these individuals and hear their stories.

One morning, while sitting on the crowded train, I struck up a conversation with a young woman seated nearby.

'Excuse me,' I began, 'I couldn't help but notice that your commute seems quite lengthy. How do you find living in Brampton?'

She glanced up from her book, and after a moment of suspicion, she responded, 'It's all right, I guess. My parents insisted I stay with or at least not far from our relatives, and moreover, this area is still more affordable than others.' She echoed the sentiment of the young man I had met earlier.

---

[1] GO Transit is a regional public transit system serving the Greater Golden Horseshoe region of Ontario, Canada. Their distinctive green and white trains carry a million passengers every week.

I probed her further, 'Are there any particular challenges that you face here?'

Her expression grew solemn, and she leaned in slightly as if confiding a secret. 'Well, the rent can be a real burden. We usually must share apartments with multiple people to make it affordable. My current place is cramped with three others, but it's the only way to keep the costs down.'

I nodded empathetically, realizing that affordability was a constant concern for newcomers. 'Do you ever face discrimination or mistreatment?' I asked cautiously.

She sighed, her eyes reflecting a mix of frustration and resignation. 'Not necessarily from outsiders, but from within our community. Some of the older folks here think they're entitled to treat us poorly because they've been here longer. It's disheartening, to say the least.'

As we continued our conversation, it became clear that she, too, had experienced the divide within the community. It seemed that the struggle to find affordable housing and acceptance were shared experiences among these young immigrants.

Over the following weeks, I engaged in more conversations with fellow passengers on the GO train, each revealing their unique stories and challenges. I embarked on numerous journeys along this route, so much so that during this time, Valerie, a wonderfully kind lady employed by GO Trains at Union Station, began to recognize me. I grew to rely on her, as each time I needed to know the ever-changing platform for the train, I would confidently approach her for assistance.

Among the people I met and spoke to, there was a young man studying engineering who shared how he had to juggle part-time jobs to make ends meet, all the while trying to excel in his studies. Another passenger, a recent graduate, spoke of the pressure to secure a job within his field while dealing with the high cost of living in Brampton, 'I worked at a Tim Hortons while I was a student, but I am a graduate now. I need to find work in my field. My points for the Express Entry Scheme or the Provincial Nominee Programme will not increase if I don't do that. I am thinking of moving to a remote area where it will be easier to secure such a job. In any case, I want to move out of this area where I am made to feel unwanted, even though I will have to leave my friends behind.'

It wasn't just financial burdens that weighed them down. Many mentioned the emotional toll of feeling like outsiders within their community, where some of the established members treated them with disdain or condescension. These encounters painted a vivid picture of the complexities and struggles faced by the new Indian immigrants.

As my conversations continued, a recurring theme emerged – the overcrowded basements and the skyrocketing rents. The desperate search for affordable housing had led to basements that used to rent for $900 being crammed with eight students, each paying $600 a month. It was a telling sign of the lengths these young individuals had to go to just to find a place to live. The house owners were making four times the money while providing sub-standard facilities.

One evening, during an exceptionally crowded train ride, I found myself standing next to a group of young men, deep in conversation about their experiences. Emboldened by their camaraderie, I decided to join in.

'Excuse me,' I interjected, 'I couldn't help but overhear your conversation. It sounds like you've faced quite a few challenges since coming to Canada.'

The young men exchanged glances and then welcomed me into their discussion. One of them, with a hint of frustration, explained, 'It's not easy, you know. We came here with dreams of a better life, but the reality can be harsh.' Another chimed in, 'The members of our community who moved in earlier than us sometimes make it even harder. They treat us like we don't belong.'

I found myself pondering a different facet of this complex narrative – the perceptions and stereotypes regarding the newer immigrants that had taken root among some earlier settlers.

'Surely there must be some reason for people to believe that the present lot of immigrants are in Canada for all the wrong reasons?' I mused one day during a conversation with a group of young men and women on the train.

The response was immediate and laced with a touch of humor. 'Well, you see,' one of them began, 'it's not that there's smoke without fire. It's more like there's a lot of smoke when you put too many students together, and sometimes, they do light up a little fire.'

Laughter rippled through the group as they exchanged knowing glances. It was clear that they had encountered these stereotypes before and were ready to debunk them.

'Canada invites students in large numbers,' another chimed in. 'And it's a well-known fact all over the world that when an 18-year-old moves out of their parents' house, they suddenly discover newfound freedom. They want to experiment, express themselves, and feel more of everything.'

A sly smile played on one young woman's lips as she added, 'Not everyone can handle this newfound freedom with maturity. Then there's the good old peer pressure. They want to impress the opposite sex.'

The group burst into laughter again, nodding in agreement. 'It's the same with students who come to Chandigarh from Punjab and Himachal Pradesh, isn't it?' one of them asked. 'It's the same with white students in Canadian universities. But the Punjabi media here doesn't seem concerned about them. They never report unruly incidents involving non-Punjabis. You can see where their focus is.'

I couldn't help but chuckle at their candid assessment of the situation. It was evident that they were well aware of the biases and selective reporting that sometimes perpetuated stereotypes. They continued, shedding light on another aspect of the issue.

'Some kids, whose parents back in India are rich, aren't motivated to struggle the way we do,' one of them said. 'They're not interested in staying in Canada after their studies and doing back-breaking work. Their parents send them here for the stamp of international education to increase their value in the marriage market back home.'

I was taken aback, not because I was unaware of this reason for educating children in Canada, but because I didn't expect the younger generation to be so informed about it as no one ever says it out loud or accepts it. They went on to explain that these students often cared little about being considerate towards others or following rules.

'The sad part,' one of them added, 'is that they make friends who aren't from such rich backgrounds and become the rich guy's *chamcha*.'[2] Laughter mixed with a hint of irony filled the air. 'These chamchas have a lot to lose if they go astray,' one of them continued. 'Unlike the person they're following, they get carried away, doing their boss's bidding because he buys them liquor, has a car to drive around in, and they think they've become the crème de la crème.'

There was a collective sigh of understanding among the group. 'They end up getting in trouble sooner or later,' one of them concluded. 'And when the law starts closing in, the rich guy catches the next flight back home, leaving his poorer friends to face the heat over here. Their parents' hard-earned money is now at stake.'

As the train rolled on, I reflected on the layers of complexity that defined the immigrant experience. Stereotypes based on

---

[2] A Hindi word for a follower or underling of a powerful person, especially a servile or unimportant one, who has an excessive willingness to serve or please the boss.

partial truths often fail to capture the full spectrum of individual journeys and aspirations. The humor and candor of these young men and women served as a reminder that while challenges and missteps existed, it was essential to recognize the diversity of experiences within the community.

Amid my continued exploration of the experiences of young Indian immigrants in Canada, I had the privilege of meeting an extraordinary young woman during one of my train journeys. Her story resonated deeply with me, shedding light on the remarkable determination and resilience of these newcomers.

She was a bright young girl with an air of confidence that was unmistakable. It didn't take long for her to open up about her journey. 'I've always been the topper of my class throughout my school life,' she proudly told me. Her English was impeccable, a testament to her dedication to her education even though she was from a small town in Punjab.

As our conversation unfolded, I learned that financial constraints had overshadowed her decision to come to Canada for a two-year diploma. Her father, despite his best efforts, could not afford to pay for a four-year undergraduate course. Nevertheless, she had made the most of her time, securing a job and attaining Permanent Resident (PR) status in Canada.

Her dream, however, reached far beyond her current achievements. She had recently been accepted into a top Canadian university with the goal of becoming an aerospace engineer. Her ambition was nothing short of inspiring, and she spoke of it with unwavering determination.

Back home, her relatives had questioned her parents about her pursuit of further education. 'Why is she still studying if she already has PR?' they would ask. 'Why not just get a job?'

While her parents supported her aspirations and stood by her decision, her relatives in Canada held a different perspective, constantly pressuring her parents to change their minds. She confided in me, 'I had to move out of my relatives' place because it became an unwelcoming environment, despite my paying rent and even for the food.'

Listening to her story, I couldn't help but admire her strength and resilience. She had chosen a path less traveled, one that demanded immense dedication and belief in herself. I was convinced that someday, this young woman would achieve greatness, and people like me would be honored to be photographed with her.

As our conversation continued, she touched upon the role of the Canadian Punjabi media in their lives. 'We thought we could seek guidance and information from the media of our community,' she explained. 'But instead, their message to us is "go back". They seem to be playing to the galleries, as the older migrants are the majority in their audience.'

Her words resonated deeply, echoing the concerns raised by others whom I had spoken to. 'In fact,' she continued, 'many of the Punjabi media personalities are also from the older generation of immigrants. They seem to feel threatened by our presence here.'

She went on to describe the media's tendency to blow out of proportion any mistake made by young Punjabi immigrants. 'If the police arrest some Punjabi youths, it becomes cannon fodder for them,' she lamented. 'They show those images over and over again, perpetuating stereotypes.'

I nodded in understanding, knowing that sensationalism in media was not unique to any one community. 'But,' I asked, 'what about the majority of young Punjabi immigrants who are hardworking and dedicated to making a difference in their lives and the lives of their families back home?' She smiled warmly, her eyes filled with determination.

'That's the story that often goes untold,' she said. 'Yes, there may be a few who make mistakes, but they are a tiny percentage. Most of us are here to build a better future through hard work and dedication.'

Our conversation continued, and it became clear that this

young woman was not only intelligent but also an eloquent advocate for her community. Her dreams of becoming an aerospace engineer were not just personal ambitions but a testament to the potential of immigrants like her who had come to Canada in search of a better life.

Her story served as a powerful reminder that the immigrant experience was not defined by adversity alone but also by the incredible strength and determination of those who dared to dream. In a land of opportunity and diversity, their voices deserve to be heard, and their dreams deserve to be realized.

Amidst the numerous conversations during my train rides, one discussion stood out as profoundly enlightening. It was with a 30-year-old engineer who had just landed a dream job, his spirits soaring when we met. His perspective on the matter shed new light on the discrimination faced by newcomers at the hands of earlier immigrants.

He was unexpectedly candid. 'These guys want to believe that they've become white,' he began, his tone tinged with both frustration and amusement. 'They yearn to mimic them, to behave like them, and in doing so, they denounce us in an attempt to gain acceptance into that camp.'

His words struck a chord within me, resonating with the notion of assimilation and superiority that had roots in history. 'But,' I inquired, 'isn't that camp a relic of the past? A time when White Canada was still adjusting to the presence of Asians?'

He nodded in agreement. 'Exactly! In the past couple of decades, Canada has moved forward. It's these people who remain trapped in a time warp, clinging to outdated ideals and attitudes. They invest their time and energy in speaking against us, convincing themselves that they are somehow superior.

'They gather in their exclusive groups, spewing derogatory remarks about us, and everyone nods in agreement. It's a cycle of validation and elation. They seem to derive a sense of achievement from believing they occupy a higher stratum within our community.'

This conversation stirred memories of William Dalrymple's book *White Mughals,* which chronicled the British officers of the late eighteenth and early nineteenth centuries in India. These men, enamored by Indian culture, would dress like the Indian nobility, sport beards and mustaches, smoke the *hookah,* and adopt Indian customs. They looked down upon the newcomers who hadn't 'orientalised' themselves enough. It was true for not only the British but also the Portuguese in Goa. Here is a passage from that book[3] where Dalrymple talks about the Portuguese behaving like Indian nobility:

> By 1560, the Portuguese grandees of Goa dressed ostentatiously in silks, shielding themselves with umbrellas, never leaving their houses except accompanied by vast retinues of slaves and servants. Travellers reported how the Goan aristocracy kept harems and that even the Christian women wore Indian clothes inside the house and lived as if in purdah, 'little seene abroad'. If they had to go out, they did so veiled or in modestly covered palanquins.
>
> Their menfolk chewed betel nut, ate rice (but only with their right hand) and drank arrack; they rubbed themselves with 'sweet sanders', and their hospital doctors prescribed the old Hindu panacea of cow urine three times a day to their patients 'in order to recover their color, one glass in the morning, one at midday, and one in the evening'.
> They drank water from the pot in the Indian fashion and touch it not with their mouths, but the water running from the spout falleth into their mouthes, never spilling a drop ... and when any man commeth newly from Portingall, and then beginneth to drink after this manner, because he is not used to this kinde of drinking, he spilleth it in his bosome, wherein they take

[3] Page 12

great pleasure and laugh at him, calling him Reynol, which is a name given in jest to such as newlie come from Portingall.

The parallels were striking. Just as the Europeans had strived to embrace Indian culture to gain acceptance, some of the earlier immigrants in Canada seemed to mimic the prevailing culture to fit in. The desire for assimilation took peculiar forms.

This newfound understanding clarified the complexities I was dealing with in my exploration of the immigrant experience. The term 'brown goras' resonated in my mind. In the Indian context, *goras* refers to the whites, who for centuries were the British, Portuguese, and French. It was a term that had once symbolized colonialism, and here in Canada, it had evolved into a symbol of those who sought to adopt a perceived 'white' way of life.

I found another term particularly apt and amusing: the use of the name 'coconut' by new immigrants to describe the older ones, as a coconut is brown on the outside but white on the inside. Kabir Mann, a young immigrant I met in British Columbia, chuckled when I inquired about the usage of this term and responded, 'Yes, it's quite commonly used here.' While it might come across as banter and humor, the ultimate outcome may not be as light-hearted as it initially appears.

With every conversation, my understanding of the challenges faced by these new Indian immigrants grew deeper. They were resilient, determined, and willing to overcome every obstacle in their path. Yet, they deserved more than just survival; they deserved a chance to thrive in a land that promised them opportunity and acceptance.

As these journeys came to an end, I carried with me not only the stories of these brave individuals but also a renewed commitment to shed light on their struggles and advocate for change. It was a journey of discovery, and I knew that their voices deserved to be heard.

Canada: A Land of Diverse Migrations

Recognizing the importance of seeking the perspectives of earlier settlers, I embarked on a journey to delve into the intricacies of Canadian migration and explore the challenges confronted by different generations of migrants, probing whether some had faced fewer hurdles than others. Fortunately, I was staying near the Toronto Reference Library, adjacent to the Bloor-Yonge station, which was a part of the Toronto Public Library system and provided me with invaluable access to meticulously curated reference books and research materials. These resources were instrumental in unraveling the complexities of each wave of emigration to Canada, and I share those insights that are most pertinent to our quest.

What's migration? It's when people pack their bags and move to a new neighborhood, town, or even a different country in search of new adventures or better lives. Migration isn't just about people on the move; it's a mega-influencer of cultures, economics, and societies worldwide. Humans have forever been nomadic, and this wanderlust has spread languages, cultures, and ideas to all corners of the globe.

Immigrants aren't just passengers on this journey; they're the fuel for economic growth, the spice in a cultural stew, and the sparks of innovation. As we reflect on these historic migrations, we celebrate the courage and determination of those who dared to explore the unknown, leaving an enduring mark on our shared history. The twentieth century saw massive migration waves.

People were jet-setting for better opportunities, escaping tough times, or seeking refuge. This movement turned our world into a true melting pot.

Canada is a unique example, and its story of migration is fascinating. Its rich cultural tapestry is a testament to the waves of migrations that have shaped the nation over centuries. From early European settlers to more recent arrivals from all corners of the globe, Canada's history is a mosaic of diverse cultures and peoples. Let us delve into the various waves of migration that have contributed to Canada's multicultural identity.

Early European Settlers: The Founders of a New World

The story of migration to Canada began with the arrival of European settlers who ventured across the Atlantic Ocean in the early sixteenth century. These pioneers braved treacherous seas and harsh wilderness to establish a foothold in the New World. French and British explorers, such as Jacques Cartier and John Cabot, set the stage for a centuries-long European presence in North America.

The Founders of a New World

The early European migrations to Canada were marked by a complex interplay of motivations, ranging from economic aspirations to religious fervor. However, they were not without their challenges, including the deep-seated suspicion and tensions that existed between Catholic and Protestant groups. Additionally, it's crucial to acknowledge the profound harm inflicted upon the Indigenous peoples because of European trade, wars, and the introduction of devastating diseases.

Religious Rifts—Catholic vs. Protestant

One of the defining features of European migration to Canada during the sixteenth and seventeenth centuries was the religious divide that ran deep within the European continent. This division was primarily between Catholic and Protestant groups, and it found its way into the New World.

Catholic settlers, mainly of French origin, established settlements in areas such as Quebec. The French explorers, led by Samuel de Champlain, were motivated by both economic interests, such as the fur trade, and a desire to spread Catholicism. The establishment of Quebec City in 1608 marked the beginning of a French-Catholic presence in Canada.

On the other side of the religious spectrum, British Protestants, influenced by the Reformation, established settlements in places like Newfoundland and the Atlantic provinces. They, too, were driven by economic incentives and a desire for religious freedom. The town of St. John's, founded in 1583, was among the first British settlements in North America.

The religious differences between these groups often led to suspicion and, at times, hostility. The French-Catholic settlers and British Protestants viewed each other with deep suspicion, with tensions occasionally erupting into conflicts. The Battle of Quebec in 1759, a pivotal moment in Canadian history during the Seven Years' War, underscored the religious and political tensions between these groups.

Impact on Indigenous Peoples

While the European settlers brought with them their religious, cultural, and economic aspirations, they inflicted significant harm upon the Indigenous peoples of Canada. The clash of cultures between European settlers and Indigenous nations resulted in profound consequences.

European trade practices, particularly the fur trade, had a lasting impact on Indigenous communities. While trade provided access to many valuable European goods, it also disrupted traditional Indigenous economies and created dependencies on European goods. The fur trade, driven by European demand for beaver pelts, led to the decimation of beaver populations and altered the ecosystem.

Moreover, the introduction of European diseases, such as smallpox, had devastating effects on Indigenous populations. Lack of immunity to these diseases resulted in widespread epidemics, decimating the Indigenous communities. This demographic catastrophe forever changed the balance of power between Indigenous nations and European settlers. The desire for land and resources also drove European settlers to engage in conflicts and wars with Indigenous nations. The Beaver Wars in the seventeenth century, for instance, were marked by violent clashes between Indigenous peoples, British and French settlers, and their respective Indigenous allies. These conflicts further disrupted Indigenous societies and led to the displacement of many Indigenous communities from their ancestral lands.

Since it's not feasible to encapsulate the entire history of diverse migrations to Canada in a single chapter, my endeavor here is to provide a concise overview of key milestones, especially those pertinent to this book.

Ukrainian Migration to Saskatchewan: Transforming the Grand Prairies

The Ukrainian migration to Canada stands out as a compelling and transformative chapter in the nation's history. This migration was necessitated by a combination of factors, including economic hardship and political unrest in Ukraine. It also occurred during a time when Canada was shunning non-white migrations, as detailed in the next section. In contrast to people of color, Ukrainians were considered white by Canadian immigration officials and had an easier time gaining entry.

The late nineteenth and early twentieth centuries were a challenging period for many Ukrainians. Ukraine, then a part of the Russian Empire, faced political instability, economic hardship, and widespread poverty. The promise of fertile land and economic opportunities abroad, particularly in the Canadian Prairies, attracted many Ukrainians to consider emigration.

Canada, with vast expanses of undeveloped land, was actively seeking settlers to cultivate its western regions. In response to the push factors in Ukraine and the pull factors in Canada, a significant wave of Ukrainian migration began in the late nineteenth century. The Ukrainians, skilled in wheat cultivation, played a pivotal role in transforming the Grand Prairies into Canada's breadbasket. Their dedication to farming, along with their use of innovative techniques, helped Canada become a major exporter of wheat and other grains. They brought with them a rich cultural heritage, including traditional folk music, dance, and cuisine, which have left a lasting imprint on Canadian culture.

By 2021, Canada's Ukrainian-origin population had grown significantly. Over 1.4 million Canadians had Ukrainian heritage, making it one of the largest ethnic groups in the country. This diaspora has made remarkable contributions to various aspects of Canadian society, including politics, education, and the arts.

However, it's important to note that the welcome extended to Ukrainian migrants was not without its challenges, largely due to the prevailing immigration policies of the time. While Ukrainian migrants were allowed to come to Canada, they still faced significant difficulties and obstacles during the immigration process and their settlement in Canada. Canada at that time favored immigrants from certain regions, primarily Western Europe and discriminated against those from other parts of the world, influenced by racial and ethnic biases.

Shunning of Migrations of People of Colour: The Komagata Maru Incident

Canada's restrictive immigration policies that favored Western European immigrants while discouraging the arrival of people of color are exemplified by the *Komagata Maru* incident of 1914. The *Komagata Maru,* a Japanese steamship, arrived in Vancouver, carrying 376 passengers, primarily Sikh and Punjabi immigrants from India. They sought to enter Canada, but they were met with resistance. The Canadian immigration authorities, citing the continuous journey regulation, denied entry to most passengers, and the ship was forced to return to India. This incident highlighted the stark racial discrimination faced by non-white immigrants attempting to settle in Canada during this era.

Upon its arrival in Canadian waters, specifically at Coal Harbour in Burrard Inlet, approximately 200 meters (220 yards) from the Canadian Pacific Railway (CPR) Pier A, the *Komagata Maru* faced the distressing reality of being denied permission to dock. The initial encounter with the ship in Vancouver involved the immigration officer Fred 'Cyclone' Taylor. While Prime Minister of Canada, Robert Borden, deliberated on the course of action regarding the ship, the Conservative Premier of British Columbia, Richard McBride, adamantly declared that the passengers would not be permitted to disembark. HH Stevens, a Conservative Member of Parliament, took it upon himself to organize a public meeting opposing the disembarkation of the ship's passengers and strongly urged the government to prevent the ship from remaining in Canadian waters. Stevens collaborated closely with immigration official Malcolm RJ Reid to keep the passengers offshore. Reid's unyielding stance, backed by Stevens, resulted in the mistreatment of those on board the ship and prolonged its departure, a situation that persisted until the federal Minister of Agriculture, Martin Burrell, Member of Parliament for Yale—Cariboo, intervened.

Within Canada, South Asian Canadians who were already settled in the country initiated 'shore committees' led by figures such as Husain Rahim (of Gujarati-Canadian descent), Muhammad Akbar (of Punjabi-Canadian descent), and Sohan Lal Pathak. These committees were formed to protest the decision that denied entry to the passengers of the *Komagata Maru*. Protest meetings were convened both in Canada and the United States. At one such gathering held at Dominion Hall in Vancouver, the attendees passed a resolution stating that if the passengers were not allowed entry into Canada, Indo-Canadians should accompany them back to India with the intent of inciting a rebellion or *ghadar*. A British government agent who had infiltrated this meeting promptly alerted government officials in London and Ottawa, informing them that supporters of the Ghadar Party were among the ship's passengers.

The shore committee managed to raise $22,000 as an initial payment for chartering the ship and initiated a lawsuit on behalf of Munshi Singh, one of the passengers, under the legal counsel of J Edward Bird. On 6 July, the full bench of the British Columbia Court of Appeal issued a unanimous judgment stating that according to new orders-in-council, they had no authority to interfere with the decisions made by the Department of Immigration and Colonization. Responding to the mounting frustration among the passengers, they took control of the ship from the Japanese captain on 19 July. Subsequently, the Canadian Government ordered the harbor tug *Sea Lion* to push the ship out to sea forcibly. On the following day, *The Sun*, a Vancouver newspaper, reported that 'Howling masses of Hindus showered policemen with lumps of coal and bricks ... it was like standing underneath a coal chute'.

Ultimately, Canada permitted the entry of merely twenty passengers due to various factors: the ship's violation of exclusion laws, the passengers' inability to meet the necessary financial criteria, and their failure to embark on a direct voyage from India. Consequently, the ship was compelled to reverse its course and commence its journey back to Asia on 23 July. The *Komagata Maru's* return to India culminated on 27 September when the vessel reached Calcutta. Upon its arrival in the harbor, a British gunboat intercepted the ship, leading to the detention of its passengers. In the eyes of the British Raj, those aboard the *Komagata Maru* were not just individuals who had admitted to breaking the law, but they were also perceived as potentially dangerous political agitators. The British Government harbored suspicions that both white and South Asian radicals were exploiting this incident to incite rebellion among South Asians in the Pacific Northwest.

As the ship docked at Budge Budge, the police attempted to apprehend Baba Gurdit Singh and around twenty other men who were seen as leaders by the authorities. It led to resistance to the arrest, and one of Baba Gurdit Singh's associates assaulted a policeman, triggering a disturbance. The situation escalated to the point where shots were fired, resulting in the tragic death of 19 passengers. Some individuals managed to escape, but the remaining passengers were either taken into custody or returned to their respective villages and subjected to village arrest throughout the duration of the First World War. This unfortunate episode came to be known as the Budge Budge Riot.

Chinese Immigrants and Their Contributions

Chinese migration to Canada has a long and complex history, marked by challenges and triumphs. From the construction of the Canadian Pacific Railway (CPR) to their invaluable contributions to Canadian society today, Chinese immigrants have left an indelible mark on the country.

Chinese immigration to Canada began in earnest during the mid-nineteenth century, with the arrival of Chinese laborers recruited to work on the construction of the CPR. They played a pivotal role in connecting Canada from coast to coast, a monumental feat that shaped the nation's economic and political landscape. The work was grueling, and the conditions were often harsh. Chinese laborers faced discrimination, low wages, and dangerous working conditions. Yet, their unwavering dedication and hard work helped complete the CPR, a project of immense national importance. In 1885, the Canadian government imposed the Chinese Head Tax, a fee that Chinese immigrants had to pay upon arrival. It was increased in 1903 and 1904, making it financially burdensome for Chinese families to reunite in Canada.

This discriminatory policy culminated in the Chinese Immigration Act of 1923, also known as the Chinese Exclusion Act. It effectively barred Chinese immigration to Canada for over two decades until its repeal in 1947. During this period, the Chinese Canadian community faced considerable hardship, including family separations and limited economic opportunities.

Despite the adversities they faced, Chinese immigrants and their descendants have made remarkable contributions to Canadian society. Chinese Canadians are an integral part of the nation's cultural fabric, enriching Canada with their traditions, cuisine, and arts. In the realm of business and entrepreneurship, Chinese Canadians have excelled. They have established thriving businesses, contributed to innovation, and played a pivotal role in the development of Canada's economy. Prominent Chinese Canadian entrepreneurs, such as David Lam and Jim Treliving, have made significant contributions to the business landscape.

Furthermore, Chinese Canadians have been active in civic engagement and politics, with many individuals holding positions of leadership and advocating for social justice and civil rights.

By 2021, the Chinese Canadian community had grown significantly, with over 1.8 million people of Chinese origin residing in Canada. Their contributions span various fields, including education, healthcare, technology, and the arts, making them an integral part of Canada's multicultural tapestry.

Japanese Immigrants and World War II

The story of Japanese immigrants in Canada is marked by both contributions to the nation's development and a dark chapter of discrimination during World War II. Japanese Canadians, like other immigrant groups, have played a vital role in shaping Canada's cultural and economic landscape.

Japanese immigration to Canada began in the late nineteenth century, primarily to British Columbia. Many of the Japanese immigrants initially worked in industries such as logging, mining, and fishing. However, a significant number of Japanese Canadians found their calling in agriculture, particularly in the fertile lands of the Fraser Valley. Japanese Canadians became renowned for their agricultural expertise, cultivating a wide range of crops, including strawberries, blueberries, and various vegetables. Their contributions to Canadian agriculture were instrumental in making British Columbia a significant producer of fresh produce.

Tragically, the contributions of Japanese Canadians were overshadowed by a grave injustice during World War II. Following the attack on Pearl Harbor in 1941 and the subsequent declaration of war between Canada and Japan, the Canadian government initiated a policy of internment and forced relocation of Japanese Canadians.

Under the War Measures Act, over 22,000 Japanese Canadians, many of whom were Canadian citizens, were forcibly removed from their homes on the west coast of Canada. They were relocated to internment camps in remote areas and subjected to harsh living conditions. The internment had devastating consequences, leading to the loss of property, livelihoods, and personal freedoms for Japanese Canadians. Families were separated, and their lives were upended. It remains a dark chapter in Canada's history and a stark violation of civil liberties.

In the decades following World War II, there was a growing recognition of the injustice done to Japanese Canadians. Efforts were made to acknowledge and rectify these wrongs. In 1988, the Canadian government issued an official apology for the internment and announced compensation for survivors and their families, an important step toward reconciliation and healing.

In the post-war years, Japanese Canadians rebuilt their lives and became active participants in Canadian culture, politics, and the economy. Many individuals of Japanese descent have excelled in fields such as business, academia, sports, and the arts.

The Early Indian Migrants

Indian migrants, primarily from the Punjab region, arrived in Canada in waves, seeking employment opportunities and a better future for their families. Their journey, marked by challenges and achievements, reflects the broader story of immigration to Canada. The early Indian migration to Canada can be traced back to the late nineteenth century when the British Empire included India as one of its largest colonies. Indian migrants, primarily from the Punjab region, initially arrived on the west coast of Canada, particularly in British Columbia. They were often recruited as laborers for various industries, including agriculture, forestry, and construction.

Along with the Chinese, one of the earliest and most significant contributions of Indian laborers was in the construction of the CPR. While it is difficult to provide an estimate of how many Indians worked there, it is estimated to be in several thousands. Their dedication and hard work in grueling conditions were instrumental in completing the railway.

Despite their contributions to Canada's infrastructure, Indian migrants faced significant discrimination and challenges, like the *Komagata Maru* incident. In addition to their work on the CPR, Indian immigrants played a significant role in the development of Canada's agriculture sector, finding employment as laborers and farm workers in the fertile regions of British Columbia and the Prairie provinces. They cultivated crops such as lumber, fruits, and vegetables, helping to expand Canada's agricultural output.

Indian immigrants also made their mark in various industries, including logging and forestry, where their labor was crucial to the growth of these sectors. Their work met the increasing demand for timber and wood products in Canada and beyond.

The Bigger Wave of Indian Migrants to Canada

There was a significant wave of Indian immigrants to Canada in the late 1960s and early 1970s. This period marked a notable increase in immigration from India to Canada, driven by several factors. A key factor was the change in Canada's immigration policy in the late 1960s.

The removal of racial and ethnic preferences from immigration policy occurred through the introduction of the Immigration Regulations of 1962 and the Immigration Act of 1967, which came into effect on 1 February 1968. These changes marked a significant shift in Canadian immigration policy and laid the foundation for a more inclusive and non-discriminatory approach to immigration.

Prior to these changes, Canada had a racially discriminatory immigration policy that favored applicants from certain countries (predominantly of European origin) while restricting immigration from other regions, including Asia, Africa, and the Caribbean. This system was often referred to as the 'White Canada' policy.

The key changes brought about by the Immigration Regulations of 1962 and the Immigration Act of 1967 included:

Introduction of a Points System

Instead of prioritizing applicants based on their country of origin or ethnicity, the new policy introduced a Points System that assessed potential immigrants based on factors such as age, education, language proficiency, work and professional experience, and adaptability. This system allowed individuals from a wide range of countries to qualify for immigration based on their individual merit.

Family Reunification

The new policy emphasized family reunification, allowing Canadian citizens and permanent residents to sponsor family members for immigration regardless of their country of origin.

Humanitarian Considerations

The policy also introduced provisions for refugees and individuals in need of humanitarian protection, emphasizing Canada's commitment to providing refuge to those facing persecution or danger in their home countries.

Elimination of Racial and Ethnic Discrimination

The most significant change was the removal of racial and ethnic preferences in the selection of immigrants. The new policy explicitly prohibited discrimination based on race, ethnicity, or national origin.

These changes were part of Canada's efforts to create a more inclusive and egalitarian immigration system that focused on the skills and contributions of individuals rather than their racial or ethnic backgrounds. Additionally, Canada's economy was growing during this time and needed skilled workers and professionals to fill labor shortages in various sectors.

The Point System gave more points to people with a job offer. This job offer could be from a farm or a packing house where fruits would be packed for dispatch to retail stores.

There was no formal English proficiency test that these people had to pass in the 1970s like the present generation of wannabes must. The specific English proficiency testing system that exists today, such as the International English Language Testing System (IELTS) or the Canadian English Language Proficiency Index Program (CELPIP), did not exist in their current form during that time. Instead, language proficiency assessment in the 1970s and earlier typically involved an interview conducted by a Canadian immigration official or visa officer. This assessment aimed to determine the applicant's ability to communicate in English or French. They were expected to find their way around, so to say, without being proficient in the language. The assessment process could vary depending on the discretion of the immigration officer and the specific circumstances of the applicant.

The point is that these people, in general, were low on English speaking skills and even education. A vast majority of them were employed as farmhands, laborers in the road or building construction and packing houses, and the stronger among them were employed in the lumber mills.

When one knows about the history of Canadian migration, one realizes that for the Indians who entered the country in the late 1960s and the 1970s, the going was the easiest in comparison to the migrants who came before them and the ones who arrived after 1989, when the IELTS exam was introduced as an English language proficiency test. In fact, there are many students and immigrants from India today who, being bilingual, are proficient in both English and French.

Immigration to Canada was extremely difficult before 1967, especially for South Asians. That is not to say that they had it easy after reaching here. They had to work hard picking apples, which used to be a difficult task in those days as the apple trees could reach a height of 20 feet. Canada has since modified the apple tree to be short and flat, going up only seven feet and not requiring any ladders to pick the fruit. Often, couples would work in the farms and later in the packing houses, seeking more than the usual eight hours of work per day and working weekends as well. The men worked in the lumber mills, which was extremely hard work, and they worked in extremely low temperatures, which they were not used to. They continued such work for thirty-odd years in many cases. A few of them worked as taxi drivers for an extended period without owning their own taxis, and it took them a considerable amount of time before they could afford to purchase one of their own. They struggled with the language, and the majority of them still feel uneasy speaking English, even after residing in the country for nearly five decades.

Despite the hardships they endured and their remarkable determination to overcome obstacles, their immigration process was comparatively less challenging than that of present-day immigrants and those who arrived before 1967. It is crucial that we shed light on this aspect to ensure they do not forget the concessions they enjoyed and, perhaps, gain a greater appreciation for the current generation of immigrants. During that era, the system did not impose mandatory minimum educational qualifications or skill requirements, as is the case for contemporary immigrants. They weren't obligated to possess any prior work experience in their specific field, a condition now demanded by the Express Entry system. They were engaged in occupations such as harvesting apples and strawberries, which was unrelated to their past experiences, as these fruits were alien to their homeland. Even most of them who became taxi drivers learned that skill in Canada as back in the day, they couldn't afford cars back home, whereas the present generation comes from households that have had cars for the last two decades if not more. Hence, most of them arrived without significant skills or formal education. All they possessed, and all that Canada demanded, was a determination to labor for 60 hours a week, regardless of the weather, time of day or night, or the working conditions. This, of course, they did.

The Other Side of the Story

As I prepared to interview the people who had left an indelible mark on the lives of my young friends, I couldn't help but feel a sense of reverence and curiosity. These were the hardworking Punjabis whose stories of perseverance had echoed in the alleys of my childhood. They had embarked on a journey to Canada with mere dollars in their pockets, a dream in their hearts, and an unshakable determination to uplift the circumstances of their families. Their stories, like the threads of a rich tapestry, wove together tales of long hours, dark nights, and cold months.

I had known for years that many of them had never truly learned how to savor the fruits of their labor; their existence was dedicated to the well-being of their families. Yet, their sacrifices had paved the way for their children to receive a good education and opportunities they themselves could only dream of. The migration wave from the late '60s to the late '80s was different from the subsequent ones.

Each of these remarkable individuals could have penned a book detailing the struggles they endured and the triumphs they achieved. They held within them stories of relentless toil and steadfast dedication, and how they denied themselves life's simple pleasures so their loved ones could thrive. Many of them had made it a point to return temporarily to India, their homeland, and construct imposing houses, gestures that served as a testament to their success and a subtle jab at those who once regarded them as worthless and inconsequential.

Tracking down these resilient souls was not a daunting task if you knew where to find them. During the day, the parks in Brampton teemed with their presence. There, one could witness grandparents dutifully babysitting their grandchildren or simply taking a respite from the confines of their homes. These parks served as meeting grounds, where men congregated on one side and women on another. It was a chance to reconnect, relive old memories, and forge new ones.

Another venue to encounter them was the Hindu temples and Sikh gurdwaras on a serene Sunday morning. The vibrant and inclusive atmosphere during the community brunches at these places offered a glimpse into their shared camaraderie. However, I quickly discerned that religious venues were not always the ideal settings to have candid conversations. There, they presented their best selves cloaked in decorum and piety. In contrast, the parks often witnessed the occasional hip flask making an appearance as they reveled in the simple pleasure of sipping whiskey under the sun while babysitting their toddlers.

Engaging these remarkable individuals in conversation was surprisingly uncomplicated. Most of them were eager to share their life stories, their journeys, and their perspectives. They peppered conversations with more questions than answers, often delving into personal matters such as the income and marital status of their interlocutors' children, sometimes even questioning the reasons behind their offspring's unmarried status. Being an Indian, I fully anticipated these inquiries.

However, if one could maintain composure, respond with politeness, and occasionally feign ignorance, a wealth of knowledge and insight awaited. Time was their ally, a commodity they possessed in abundance since most of them had retired. These individuals exuded immense pride in their children's accomplishments, as if the sacrifices they had made were a testament to their unyielding commitment to the welfare and prosperity of their families.

In hushed tones, they spoke of their sacrifices, how they had denied themselves not just material pleasures but the simple joys of life. They had become adept at the art of saving, for they understood that frugality and thriftiness were the stepping stones to their current affluence and security. Their stories resonated with a common thread: the arduous journey from humble beginnings to the present, driven by an unwavering belief in the power of hard work, discipline, and resilience.

Approaching one such group of seasoned immigrants, I introduced myself and shared my interest in understanding their views on the new wave of arrivals. Their initial skepticism was palpable, but as I explained my intentions and genuine curiosity, they began to open up.

Some wore flowing beards and turbans, while others were clean-shaven. The women were adorned in vibrant Punjabi salwar-kameez, a beautiful fusion of tradition and modernity. I settled on a bench nearby, my curiosity piqued by the intriguing dynamics within the group. I began the conversation with a simple question to break the ice, 'How do you feel about the new crop of immigrants and students from India?'

Their responses were surprisingly laced with venom, each word dripping with disapproval. 'They are not here for studies. They have come here to migrate,' one of the elderly men declared, his eyes filled with disdain.

I attempted to remind them that they, too, had once made the journey to Canada for the same reason. They either ignored my comment or exchanged knowing glances as if sharing a secret.

'Our times were different,' said a woman, her voice tinged with nostalgia. 'We worked hard. We didn't go to nightclubs. We were not involved in crime. We didn't live in cramped-up basements.'

I decided to delve deeper, converting their statements into questions. 'Do you think they are not working hard?' I inquired.

Their response was swift and defensive.

'If they are, then they are doing it for themselves, not for us,' one man retorted, his tone unyielding.

'Why should they work for you?' I probed further.

Their eyes narrowed as they exchanged glances, but they eventually conceded, 'They shouldn't. But they should not be involved in crime.'

I pressed on, seeking evidence for their claims. 'Do you have figures on how many of them are involved in crimes?'

Their response surprised me. 'Last month, two cars got stolen,' one elderly gentleman admitted. 'We don't know who stole them, but two Punjabi kids had been caught and arrested earlier with stolen cars. We suspect that all stolen cars are their doing.'

I questioned further, attempting to bring a broader perspective. 'Canada has accepted over 100,000 Indian students and immigrants in the last year. How many do you think are involved in crime?'

Their reply was dishearteningly vague. 'The TV has reported names, many Punjabi kids involved in crime,' a woman stated firmly. I wondered aloud if it was the Punjabi media focusing on crime within their community, giving the impression that it was quite widespread.

'Perhaps the Punjabi media is concentrating on crime by Punjabis and not reporting or under-reporting any other crime. That's why it appears that they are doing all crime,' I suggested. I asked them if channels that are not focused on Punjabi content also tend to report crimes within the Punjabi community exclusively, or do they include crime reports from other communities as well?

Their response remained steadfast. 'The Punjabi media has to report on Punjabis only,' one man stated emphatically. 'We don't believe that it's a one-sided story we are being presented.'

Determined to maintain a balanced perspective, I shifted my focus to the issue of cramped basements. 'Do they own the houses where the basements are crowded, or is it your generation that is filling them for extra profits?'

For the first time, a few heads nodded in agreement. 'Some people are exploiting these kids,' an elderly woman admitted, her voice tinged with regret. 'It's not their fault entirely.'

I renewed this conversation with a glimmer of hope now, thinking that I might be able to foster empathy for the new immigrants among the elders of Brampton. However, my optimism was quickly dashed as I began to ask questions that unveiled a deeply rooted mistrust in their minds.

'Do you know how expensive it is for their parents to send them here?' I inquired. 'Many have taken loans from private lenders at extremely high interest rates and given their land as collateral. These young people are well aware of their parent's difficulties and are working hard to reduce their burden. They work night shifts so they can earn a bit extra.'

I expected nods of understanding, a recognition of the sacrifices these newcomers were making for their families. Instead, I was met with incredulous stares. One elderly gentleman shook his head and said, 'They pay bribes to get jobs.'

I was taken aback. 'Bribes? To whom?' I asked, my confusion evident.

'To the supervisors,' he replied matter-of-factly.

Naturally, I pointed out, 'But the supervisors aren't students, right? They are from among you?'

They insisted that the sheer number of students coming in was the root of the problem. I attempted to reason with them, explaining that the Canadian education system determined the vacancies in universities and colleges and the government granted that visas. These were not illegal immigrants; they were paying substantial fees and charges.

'They are giving false certificates,' one elder interjected.

I informed them that every university degree, irrespective of the country, undergoes third-party verification before a Permanent Resident certificate is granted. They dismissed it as a farce. It became increasingly evident that the young engineer's warning about them living in a time warp was accurate. When they had moved to Canada, many had done so on false guarantees and certificates, and while there might still be isolated cases, the times had changed. Services like World Education Services (WES) were now widely used for Education Credential Assessment (ECA). They seemed blissfully unaware of these developments.[4]

---

[4] Individuals seeking educational and professional opportunities across international borders encounter a complex web of requirements and regulations. One vital organization that simplifies the process and ensures that foreign qualifications are recognized and evaluated accurately is the World Education Services (WES). It is a globally recognized non-profit organization that specializes in credential evaluation and verification. The Education Credential Assessment (ECA) is a critical step for individuals planning to immigrate to Canada through various immigration pathways, such as Express Entry or Provincial Nominee Programs (PNPs). The ECA is a process through which foreign educational credentials are assessed and compared to Canadian standards to determine their equivalency in the Canadian education system. This evaluation is crucial to demonstrate an applicant's qualifications and eligibility for immigration.

Applicants submit their academic transcripts, degrees, diplomas, and other relevant documents to WES, which verifies the authenticity of these documents directly with the issuing institutions. This helps ensure the accuracy and legitimacy of the information provided by applicants. Once the documents are verified, WES assesses the foreign educational credentials and determines their Canadian equivalency. This evaluation considers factors such as the level and duration of study, grading systems, and the overall educational framework of the applicant's home country.

After completing the assessment, WES issues an official ECA report to the applicant. This report includes valuable information about the applicant's educational background and the Canadian equivalency of their credentials. It provides a clear understanding of how their foreign qualifications align with Canadian standards.

The ECA report issued by WES is widely recognized and accepted by Immigration, Refugees, and Citizenship Canada (IRCC). Applicants can use this report as part of their immigration application to demonstrate their education and qualification levels. It is especially crucial for applicants who are awarded Comprehensive Ranking System (CRS) points for their educational credentials in the Express Entry system. WES follows rigorous evaluation standards and maintains transparency in its processes. This consistency ensures that all applicants are assessed fairly, regardless of their country of origin or educational background.

WES keeps up to date with changes in educational systems worldwide. As a result, it can adapt its evaluation criteria to reflect evolving global standards, ensuring that its assessments remain accurate and relevant.

I must admit I wasn't in a comfortable position now as these men and women were not yielding. Evidently, these people had sat on these benches and not only sought but also obtained approval for their beliefs during every meeting. The more I advocated for the newcomers' position, the more aggressive they became. A gentleman in his 70s declared, 'When you go back to India, tell these kids not to come to Canada.'

Perplexed, I inquired, 'Why?'

He responded, 'Because there are no jobs.'

I countered, 'But if they don't find jobs here, they will go back after their education. They can only afford to stay if they get jobs. You don't have to tell them that. Your generation won't pay for their living here. So, what's your fear?'

A lady chimed in, 'Our children find it difficult to get jobs.'

I sighed inwardly. The age-old fear of immigrants taking jobs. Ironically, these were first-generation immigrants opposing further immigration. I persisted, 'Surely your children have had a Canadian education right from the beginning. They speak better English and understand Canadian life better than the newcomers. If they still can't secure jobs, there must be some other reason. Don't you think they need to improve their skills and abilities or maybe just have more fire in the belly?'

They replied, 'It's the large numbers they have to compete against.'

I questioned, 'Is it unfair competition?'

Their response was swift, 'These immigrants are unscrupulous.'

I probed further, 'How so?'

At first, they struggled to provide concrete examples, but when pressed, they mentioned that some immigrants were willing to give bribes for jobs and would do anything to secure employment. I inquired if they had any specific instances to support this claim, to which they responded, 'It's common knowledge.'

I couldn't help but press further, asking if there was a systemic acceptance of bribes for jobs in Canada, pointing out that if there was indeed, then the immigrants were the victims in such a scenario. However, they insisted that the newcomers were corrupting the established system.

By this point, it had become clear to me that these were imagined scenarios, born of unfounded suspicion and perpetuated as truth. The elders held these beliefs firmly, even in the absence of proof or reasonable cause for suspicion. It was time to say goodbye to them. I would have to look for some more later.

As soon as I had another opportunity, I went back to the same park but to a different area within it. The bright and sunny day seemed to energize the park, infusing it with life and laughter. As I approached the park, my heart brimming with anticipation, I encountered a burly Sikh gentleman sporting a vibrant yellow turban. He moved with surprising agility for his build, his presence commanding attention. I decided to strike up a conversation with him, eager to explore different perspectives.

With a warm smile, I began, 'You know, I've been talking to some people about the new generation immigrants here, and I've heard various opinions.'

He chuckled heartily and said, 'Ah, you city-bred educated people. Always probing where nothing needs to be probed. What is there to know about these young people? They are just burning their parents' money. They are here to find boyfriends and girlfriends. To be away from their parents' control.'

Taken aback by his straightforwardness, I asked politely, 'Do you seriously believe that?'

He laughed once more, a jovial twinkle in his eye. 'Of course,' he replied confidently. 'Everyone will tell you that. Do boys and girls hold hands in the villages in India? They do here. Haven't you seen it?'

I nodded, acknowledging the observation. I didn't have the heart to tell him that nowadays, it is a common sight in India for boys and girls to hold hands in public, maybe not in the villages but certainly in the cities. He seemed emboldened by my response. 'Here, let me call my friends over, and you can ask them,' he suggested.

With that, he called out to some seniors sitting around a round-shaped table nearby. They exchanged glances and gestured for us to join them. As I took a seat among them, it became clear that this group was just as determined to voice their opinions as the previous one.

I turned to a gentleman with a white beard and a thoughtful expression. 'What do you think about the new immigrants?' I inquired.

He stroked his beard, deep in thought, and then responded, 'These young folks come here and get carried away by wrong things. I don't mind if they don't come to the gurdwara and go to the church instead. But they do neither.'

I gently countered, 'Isn't it natural for young people to try and experience life? I agree it is newfound freedom, but isn't it always difficult among all students, Indian or Canadian?'

He shook his head firmly. 'You don't know. They have parties running late into the night. Boys and girls are together. No one to check them.'

I pressed further, 'But that's student life in general. Why should these kids behave differently?'

His response was adamant. 'You should have seen our times. Our only complaint in life used to be that we were getting just 40 hours of work per week. We all wanted to work 60 hours, and indeed, we often did. This generation can't do that.'

I tried to reason that their generation had not moved in as students. These students must attend classes, submit projects, learn extra skills if possible, and handle jobs. I don't think anyone heard me.

I shifted my attention to a woman with a graceful demeanor who had been listening intently. 'What about their educational pursuits?' I asked. 'Many of them come here for higher education.'

She raised an eyebrow and replied, 'Education? Ha! They are just here for a good time. Partying, clubbing, and wasting their parents' money.'

I attempted to reason, 'But education is still important to them. They're investing in their future.'

She scoffed, 'Investing in what future? They don't even know what they want. They change their majors like they change their clothes.'

Undeterred, I continued, 'Many of them work part-time jobs to support themselves and help their families. They are aware of the financial burden on their parents.'

She waved her hand dismissively. 'Working? It's just an excuse to meet friends and have fun. We didn't have these distractions in our time.'

I turned to the burly gentleman who had initiated the conversation. 'What about their relationships? Are they not entitled to find love and companionship?'

He grinned mischievously. 'Love? They confuse love with infatuation. Back in the day, we knew what it meant to be committed, to be loyal. These kids hop from one relationship to another like it's a game.'

I persisted, 'If this poses an issue, doesn't it concern their entire generation rather than solely immigrants from India?'

His response was firm. 'The Canadian kids have rich parents. They can afford to waste time and money. These kids are here to study, not to find spouses.'

Once again, I found myself trying to bridge the gap between generations, attempting to convey the challenges and aspirations of the newcomers. It became evident that the older generation expected students from their homeland to behave like ascetics or even automatons. How could I explain to them that twenty-year-olds exhibit similar behaviors regardless of their location? While most of these young individuals are dedicated to their educational and career goals, they also engage in typical youthful activities such as dating, attending parties, and occasionally enjoying some leisure time.

Not one to give up easily, I found similar surroundings in nearby Mississauga, so I took a train for the suburb. The train pulled into the station with a familiar rumble, and I stepped onto the platform, taking in the surroundings. Mississauga was a diverse suburban oasis, a short ride from Toronto. The fact that it was on the same train line as Brampton made it an easy choice.

As I walked through the station and out onto the streets, I couldn't help but notice the mix of cultures that defined this place. Mississauga was home to a sizeable Pakistani Punjabi population, but it also welcomed Indian Punjabis. Among its 700,000 residents, 13,000 were Punjabi-speaking Indians, while about 5,000 spoke Hindi, a number dwarfed by the 6,000 Tamil speakers in town. A couple of thousand residents spoke Telugu, Malayalam, and Marathi. The Pakistani Urdu-speaking population numbered around 22,000. It was a melting pot of cultures and languages, and it fascinated me.

At this point, I was glad to discover that I wasn't alone in my quest to engage in meaningful discussions. I stumbled upon a small group of Indians, mostly in their sixties and seventies, who were unafraid to tackle uncomfortable questions. I asked the group what they thought about these newcomers, expecting a range of opinions. To my surprise, I received a unanimous response.

'They're polluting the place, overpopulating it, and living in unhygienic and cramped conditions,' they declared. However, this time, I had a lady take them on. She introduced herself as a retired schoolteacher and informed us, 'It's the greed of house owners that allows so many students to live in their houses. When they build the houses, they don't get the kitchens inspected and passed for the basement to save money. Then they add those on the sly and let out these rooms to more students than they ought to, just to make extra money without providing proper amenities.'

Her words struck a chord with the others, and several heads in the gathering nodded in agreement. Seated next to her was a man with jet-black hair that contrasted sharply with the grey around him. He leaned forward and added, 'Some of these basements don't even have an emergency or fire exit.'

While some in the group concurred with his concerns, others chimed in, saying that houses without proper exits had already received notices from the authorities. The man with the black hair shook his head, his frustration evident. 'The authorities can't get into every room,' he said, his voice tinged with exasperation.

I was relieved to see that not everyone in the room shared the same viewpoint. However, most of the group quickly dismissed the man. 'We don't force them to live like that,' the one frail old man asserted.

'At the very least, the house owners can reduce the rent, so these kids don't have to work night shifts to pay for them,' said the schoolteacher.

The replies were weak arguments but on similar lines: 'They can't expect to stay for free. They don't have manners, and they don't keep the place clean...'

As I listened to the group, I realized that their opinions were deeply rooted in their beliefs and experiences rather than an objective assessment of the situation. It struck me that change and progress often faced resistance from those who clung to their own perceptions of what was right. The complexities of immigration and integration were not easily solved by pointing fingers or placing blame. I decided to speak up, addressing the group respectfully. 'It's important to remember that these students are often far from home, trying to make a better future for themselves. They face numerous challenges, including language barriers and a lack of financial resources. While some may not maintain the highest standards of cleanliness, many are doing their best to adapt to a new environment.'

A few nods of agreement came from some of the attendees, but the older among them remained firm in their stance. 'They should still respect our rules and norms,' one of the women insisted.

I took a deep breath before responding, 'Of course, respect is essential, but it's also important for us, as a diverse community, to understand and empathize with their struggles. Many of these students are working hard to achieve their dreams, just as you all did when you first arrived in this country.'

The place fell into a contemplative silence. I could tell that my words had given some of the attendees food for thought. Perhaps there was room for change and growth in their perspectives.

As the discussion continued, I realized that the path to fostering understanding and acceptance was a long and challenging one. But the fact that we were engaging in these conversations, even if uncomfortable at times, was a promising start. Mississauga might be a diverse suburb with its fair share of issues, but it was also a place where people were willing to come together and confront the complexities of their community.

I had spent enough time in Mississauga to get a sense of how some of the older residents felt about the influx of new immigrants, particularly those from India. It was a complex issue, and I felt compelled to share my observations with a friend who had made Brampton his home for the past twenty-five years.

I remembered my friend from our college days as a brilliant young man who had a deep respect for tradition. Now, at fifty-five, he was still younger than the pioneers who had migrated to Canada in the '70s and '80s. As I sat down with him over a cup of Turkish coffee, to which he treated me in Downtown Toronto, I couldn't help but notice the change time had wrought upon him. His once jet-black hair had turned salt-and-pepper, although his body still displayed the results of regular exercise.

'So, how's life treating you in Brampton?' I asked, genuinely curious about his perspective on the evolving community.

He leaned back in his chair and sighed. 'Well, it's a different place now,' he began. 'I remember when I first came here, it was a small town, and everyone knew everyone. But now, it's different.'

I raised an eyebrow, 'How's that?'

He chuckled. 'You see, we've had so many new immigrants from India, especially Punjab, that it's almost like we've created our own version of Canada right here. Things just aren't the same anymore. The immigrants coming in now are uncouth and spoiling everything.'

I nodded as though understanding his perspective. It was clear that the demographic landscape of Brampton had shifted significantly over the years. Now, out of a total population of 680,000 in Brampton, 80,000 individuals speak Punjabi.

As our conversation flowed, my friend didn't waste any time expressing his grievances about the newcomers. 'You know,' he began, 'I recently went to a concert featuring a popular Punjabi singer, and when I went to the toilets, they were a mess. The youngsters—our youngsters—had just left them in a terrible state.'

I couldn't help but smile at his observation. 'Well, that's not unique to Brampton or any specific community,' I replied. 'Concerts all over the world tend to be messy places. Young people go there to have fun, enjoy some music, drink beer, and dance. The bathrooms are always a challenge, with long lines and less-than-ideal conditions. It's not about the color of their skin; it's just the nature of such events.'

I decided to share my own experience to drive home the point. 'You know, I attended a Bruce Springsteen concert way back in 1987, and I've been to many other concerts since then. When I was younger, I used to hold my bladder until the end of the concert. Now, well, I don't hang around that long. Why? Because the washrooms at these venues can never match up to what we'd consider clean and hygienic.'

My friend's expression shifted, and he seemed somewhat

surprised. 'You attended a concert like that?' he asked.

I nodded. 'Yes, I did. I have attended many. And I can assure you, clean toilets are a luxury rarely found at such events.'

It became evident that my friend had never experienced a pop concert before. He had been busy with his career, building a life for himself, raising a family, and fulfilling his responsibilities. The concert he attended was perhaps a rare break from his routine, and he had no previous benchmark for comparison.

I couldn't resist a playful tease. 'You see, my friend, the world of concerts is a wild one, filled with electrifying energy and passionate fans. It's a world away from our daily lives, but it comes with its own set of quirks and messiness.'

After I returned to India, our discussion continued via WhatsApp chat. My friend and I revisited the topic, and it was clear that his concerns still weighed on his mind. 'You know,' he typed, 'I understand that other communities may behave the same way during concerts, but it just feels different when it's our own community. We hold them in such high esteem.'

His words struck a chord with me. It was a common sentiment among many immigrants—they wanted their fellow countrymen to excel, to be exemplary ambassadors of their culture and heritage. My friend, too, had expectations of students from his community attending concerts and behaving as if they were attending a lecture by the head priest.

I replied, trying to offer a balanced perspective, 'It's natural to want our community members to shine, but we should also remember that they are young, just like we once were. They're navigating a new world, trying to blend their cultural roots with the expectations of their new home. It's a learning curve, and they'll find their way.'

Our conversation continued for a while longer, touching on various aspects of life in Brampton and the complexities of cultural integration. I realized that my friend's concerns, like those of the older residents in Mississauga, stemmed from a mixture of nostalgia, pride, and a genuine desire to convince themselves that they had succeeded and, indeed, become the white man whom they may have served earlier.

I couldn't help but appreciate that immigration wasn't just about relocating physically; it also involved navigating the intricate terrain of cultural evolution and mutual understanding. My friend, with his well-intentioned worries, was a testament to the ongoing dialogue between generations and the ongoing quest for harmony in the ever-evolving tapestry of multicultural societies like Brampton.

My transition from simply meeting people to delving into the intricacies of why certain groups harbor animosity towards one another when, ideally, empathy and understanding should prevail marked a pivotal shift in my journey. I returned to the hallowed halls of the Toronto Public Library, a sanctuary of knowledge. There, amidst the rows of carefully curated books, I immersed myself in the realm of psychology.

Within the pages of psychology books, I found enlightening insights into the intricate web of human emotions and behaviors that underlie intergroup conflicts. These texts offered me valuable perspectives on the psychological factors that fuel hatred, prejudice, and discrimination, shedding light on the mechanisms behind these complex phenomena. As I pored over these volumes, I began to unravel the intricate layers of human psychology, understanding the roots of animosity and the factors that hinder the emergence of empathy and understanding between different groups in society. The library became my refuge, a place where I sought answers that I share in the next chapter.

Intergroup Hatred

It may sound surprising, but I met first-generation immigrants in the United Kingdom who confessed that they voted for Brexit. They themselves came as immigrants in search of better opportunities, but they wanted the door to be shut behind them. That is exactly what is happening in Canada now. Although it may appear puzzling, that is the actual situation. Understanding the mechanisms behind intergroup hatred is crucial for addressing and mitigating these issues. Social scientists and policymakers can use this knowledge to develop interventions aimed at reducing prejudice, promoting intergroup harmony, and fostering a more inclusive society.

Psychologists have conducted studies on the phenomenon of intergroup hatred and why people may be drawn to it. One key area of research is social psychology, which explores the underlying factors that contribute to prejudice, discrimination, and hatred between different groups.

Social Identity Theory: Understanding the Roots of Intergroup Hatred

The Social Identity Theory suggests that people tend to categorize themselves and others into various social groups (e.g., based on race, religion, and nationality). They derive part of their self-esteem and identity from these groups. In this context, hating or discriminating against an out-group can boost one's self-esteem and sense of belonging within their group.

Developed by British social psychologist Henri Tajfel and his colleagues in the 1970s, the theory provides valuable insights into the dynamics of intergroup relations, prejudice, and discrimination. It offers a framework for understanding why people often identify with and favor their own social groups while simultaneously harboring negative attitudes and behaviors toward out-groups. At the heart of Social Identity Theory lies the concept that individuals derive part of their self-esteem and identity from the social groups they belong to. Moreover, it explains how the act of hating or discriminating against an out-group can boost one's self-esteem and sense of belonging within their group.

The theory posits that people have a natural tendency to categorize themselves and others into different social groups based on shared characteristics, such as race, religion, nationality, ethnicity, gender, and even more trivial factors like sports team affiliation. These groups form a crucial part of an individual's identity, providing a sense of belonging and a framework for understanding the social world. There are three key concepts here.

Social Categorization

People categorize themselves and others into various social groups. These categories can be quite fluid and context dependent. For example, a person might identify as a student when in an academic setting, as a parent when with their children, or as a fan when attending a sports event.

Social Identification

Once people categorize themselves into a particular group, they begin to identify with that group. They perceive themselves as a member of the group and incorporate the group's values, norms, and identity into their self-concept. This identification often leads to a positive evaluation of one's in-group.

Social Comparison

People tend to compare their in-groups with out-groups, which can result in acquiring a sense of superiority or inferiority. Various factors, including social status, power, and stereotypes can influence this comparison.

The Role of Self-Esteem in Social Identity Theory

One of the central ideas of Social Identity Theory is that individuals seek to maintain and enhance their self-esteem, which is their subjective evaluation of their self-worth and competence. Self-esteem is closely tied to the groups to which individuals belong. This connection between self-esteem and group membership has significant implications for understanding why people may engage in discriminatory or hateful behaviors towards out-groups.

According to the theory, people have a vested interest in viewing their group favorably to maintain or enhance their self-esteem. This positive bias towards the in-group can manifest in various ways.

In-Group Favouritism

Individuals tend to perceive their in-group more positively than out-groups. They attribute positive qualities to their group members and end up downplaying or stereotyping members of out-groups.

Out-Group Derogation

Conversely, individuals may harbor negative attitudes or stereotypes about members of out-groups. These derogatory beliefs about the out-group can serve to elevate the in-group's status and self-esteem.

The Role of Intergroup Competition

Intergroup competition plays a crucial role in understanding how hating or discriminating against an out-group can boost one's self-esteem within the context of Social Identity Theory. When groups compete for resources, status, or recognition, individuals within those groups often become more strongly identified with their in-group. The heightened identification is a natural response to the perceived threat from the competing out-groups.

Research conducted by Tajfel and Turner (1979) demonstrated that even minimal group categorizations (e.g., based on arbitrary criteria like a preference for certain paintings) could lead to in-group favoritism and out-group discrimination when people believed they were in a competitive situation. This study illustrated how individuals readily formed social identities and engaged in discriminatory behavior when group competition was introduced. Let me walk you through this experiment quickly.

Often referred to as the Minimal Group Paradigm, it was a groundbreaking study in the field of social psychology. It aimed to investigate how minimal, arbitrary group categorizations could lead to in-group favoritism and out-group discrimination under conditions of intergroup competition.

In this experiment, participants were randomly assigned to one of two minimal groups based on an arbitrary and inconsequential criterion: their preference for certain paintings by abstract artists. Importantly, the participants did not choose their groups, nor did the groups have any real significance or social relevance. The researchers ensured that the categorization was minimal, with no prior group affiliations or biases.

The participants were shown a series of paintings by different abstract artists and were asked to express their preferences by allocating points to the paintings. Unbeknownst to them, their allocations were manipulated so that they were categorized into two groups: those who preferred the paintings of artist A and those who preferred the paintings of artist B. This simple act of categorization created minimal groups.

The researchers then introduced an intergroup competition element to the experiment. Participants were informed that they would be distributing rewards (monetary points) to other participants, both from their own group (in-group) and the other group (out-group). The key condition was that participants believed they were distributing points based on group membership, even though the groups were formed based on trivial preferences for paintings.

The results of the experiment were striking. Participants consistently and significantly favored their in-group over the out-group when distributing rewards. Even though the group categorization was arbitrary and unrelated to personal characteristics or meaningful differences, participants showed a clear bias in favor of their group. They allocated more points to the in-group members and fewer points to the out-group members.

Tajfel and Turner's Minimal Group Paradigm demonstrated that people tend to exhibit in-group favoritism and out-group discrimination even when group categorizations are minimal and arbitrary. This suggests that the mere act of categorizing people into different groups can be enough to trigger intergroup biases.

The findings have important implications for understanding the roots of prejudice and discrimination in society. They suggest that social categorization and the desire for a positive social identity can drive people to favor their own group and discriminate against others, even in situations where group differences are entirely trivial. This research highlights the powerful role that social identity and group dynamics play in shaping human behavior and attitudes.

The Minimal Group Paradigm has since become a foundational study in social psychology, shedding light on the psychological mechanisms that underlie intergroup relations and helping researchers explore the complexities of prejudice, discrimination, and bias.

Boosting Self-Esteem through Out-Group Discrimination

The link between self-esteem and out-group discrimination can be understood through several mechanisms.

Enhancing In-Group Status

Discriminating against an out-group can lead to an increased perception of the in-group's status and competence. When individuals feel that their group is superior to the out-group, it bolsters their self-esteem by association.

Social Comparison

Social comparison processes are at the core of self-esteem maintenance. When individuals compare their in-group favorably to an out-group, it provides a sense of superiority, reinforcing their self-esteem. This comparative advantage can be a powerful motivator for discriminatory behaviors.

Positive Distinctiveness

Social Identity Theory posits that individuals seek to maintain a positive distinctiveness for their in-group. This means they strive for their group to be unique and superior in some way. Discriminating against out-groups can create a sense of uniqueness and distinctiveness that boosts self-esteem.

Belongingness

Engaging in discriminatory behavior can strengthen an individual's sense of belonging to their in-group. It fosters a sense of unity and solidarity among in-group members, which contributes to enhanced self-esteem.

Confirmation Bias

People tend to selectively seek and interpret information that supports their positive view of their in-group and negative view of out-groups. This confirmation bias reinforces their self-esteem by reinforcing the perceived superiority of the in-group.

Real-World Examples and Implications

Social Identity Theory's insights into the relationship between self-esteem and intergroup hatred can be observed in various real-world contexts. For instance, ethnic conflicts, religious tensions, and political rivalries often involve heightened in-group identification and out-group derogation. In these situations, individuals may dehumanize or vilify members of opposing groups to boost their own group's self-esteem and maintain a positive social identity. I observed a clear example of this when observing the elders in Brampton.

In the previous chapter, we noticed that there was also a fear of jobs being lost due to the arrival of migrants, and this is when many homeowners make more money by renting out a room to more individuals than could be previously imagined. This aspect is worth discussing further.

The Psychology of Fear, Threat, and Intergroup Hostility

Fear and threat perception plays a significant role in understanding intergroup dynamics, including hostility and prejudice. Whether real or imagined, they can profoundly impact how individuals and groups relate to one another. This psychological aspect is essential for comprehending the origin and intensification of feelings of hatred towards out-groups.

Fear is a fundamental and adaptive emotion that has evolved in humans and other animals as a response to potential dangers. This innate capacity to recognize and respond to threats has been essential for survival throughout human evolution. In modern society, fear still operates as an emotional and psychological mechanism that influences our behavior and attitudes, including how we perceive and interact with different social groups.

Perceived threat, in the context of intergroup relations, refers to the belief that an out-group poses a danger or challenge to one's own group's well-being, resources, or values. This perception of threat can arise from various sources, including economic, social, and political factors. Understanding how perceived threats affect intergroup dynamics is critical for comprehending why people may develop or intensify feelings of hostility towards out-groups.

Economic factors can be a potent source of perceived threat. When individuals or groups believe that members of an out-group are competing for the same resources, jobs, or economic opportunities, it can create a sense of insecurity and hostility, which can get exacerbated during times of economic downturns or scarcity as competition for limited resources intensifies.

Research by Robbers and Tyler (2003) suggests that economic threat can lead individuals to support policies that discriminate against out-groups or to engage in prejudiced behaviors. For example, if people believe that immigrants are taking away jobs, they may support stricter immigration policies or hold negative attitudes toward immigrant communities. This brings under the spotlight the Indian-origin Brexiters that I mentioned earlier.

Social factors, such as changes in cultural norms, values, or social hierarchies, can also generate perceived threats. When individuals perceive that the values and traditions of their in-group are being challenged or undermined by an out-group, it can lead to increased hostility. This threat can manifest as resistance to social change, the preservation of cultural identity, or the exclusion of those who are perceived as different.

For instance, when there is a perception that an out-group threatens traditional social norms, some individuals may become more resistant to inclusivity and diversity, leading to feelings of hostility or prejudice. This can be observed in debates over issues like LGBTQ+ rights, gender equality, or religious freedom. The discussions in the previous chapters amply demonstrate this.

Political factors, too, can be a potent source of perceived threat in intergroup relations. When individuals or groups perceive that an out-group's political agenda or actions threaten their own group's interests or values, it can result in heightened intergroup hostility. For example, political polarization can lead to the perception that members of opposing political parties or ideologies pose a threat to the nation's stability or well-being. This perception can contribute to increased animosity, prejudice, and even violence between different political groups.

Perceived threats, whether they originate from economic, social, or political sources, can intensify feelings of hostility and even hatred towards out-groups. When people perceive that their group's well-being or identity is at risk, it triggers a defensive response. This response may involve derogating the out-group, advocating for exclusionary policies, or even engaging in acts of outright aggression. The psychology behind this intensification of hostility is rooted in the preservation of one's group identity and self-esteem. In response to perceived threats, individuals often seek to protect their group's interests and strengthen their social identity by emphasizing differences between their in-group and the out-group.

The Brampton and Mississauga elders treated the out-group, the students arriving from India, with hostility. The students, on the other hand, were under the impression that they were walking into a new life where they would have strong support from their well-established community after years of hard work. They were in for a surprise.

Socialization, Stereotyping, Prejudice, Hatred and Cognitive Bias

The development of prejudiced attitudes, biases, and stereotypes is a complex and multifaceted process that begins early in life. Socialization—the lifelong process of learning and internalizing cultural norms, values, and behaviors—plays a pivotal role in shaping how individuals perceive and interact with different social groups. This chapter explores the critical role of socialization in the development of prejudiced attitudes and how media, family, and peer influences contribute to the formation and perpetuation of stereotypes.

The Influence of Media, Family, and Peers

Socialization is the process through which individuals acquire the knowledge, behaviors, and cultural norms of their society. It is a lifelong journey that starts in early childhood and continues throughout one's life. During this process, individuals learn how to function in their society, adopt roles, and develop a sense of identity. However, socialization isn't merely about acquiring skills; it also involves internalizing beliefs and attitudes about the world and the people in it.

Early socialization, which primarily occurs during childhood and adolescence, lays the foundation for an individual's core beliefs and values. During this formative period, children are especially receptive to external influences, absorbing information from their environment like sponges. Family, peers, and media are some of the most influential agents in shaping these early beliefs. In the Indian context, I suspect that the hatred for other religions, castes, regions, languages, and plenty more is learned at this stage. Elaborating on this with examples would be easy but lengthy and, hence, must be ignored.

Stereotypes are simplified, often exaggerated, and generalized beliefs or judgments about particular groups of people. They serve as cognitive shortcuts that help individuals make sense of the world quickly. They can be both positive and negative, but it is the negative stereotypes that are most concerning when they contribute to prejudiced attitudes and discriminatory behavior.

Stereotypes have a profound impact on how individuals perceive and interact with people from different social groups. They can influence attitudes, behaviors, and decision-making. When individuals encounter members of a group they hold negative stereotypes about, these preconceived notions can lead to bias, discrimination, and prejudice.

Media as an Agent of Socialization

Media, including television, movies, the Internet, and print, is a pervasive and powerful agent of socialization. I have dedicated the next chapter to the Punjabi media in Canada. Here, I can mention that the media provides individuals with information about the world, shapes their perceptions, and influences their attitudes and beliefs. Media exposure begins early in life, and its messages can have a lasting impact.

The media plays a significant role in reinforcing existing stereotypes or challenging them. When media perpetuates stereotypes about different social groups, it can contribute to the development of prejudiced attitudes. For example, portrayals of racial and ethnic minorities in roles that reinforce negative stereotypes can influence how people perceive and interact with these groups.

The Family as the First Socialization Agent

The family is often considered the primary agent of socialization. It is where children first learn about the world, their culture, and their place in it. Family members serve as role models, impart values, and communicate beliefs about various social groups.

Stereotypes can be passed down through generations within families. Parents and caregivers can unintentionally transmit stereotypes to children through their words, actions, and attitudes. Children may internalize these stereotypes as they learn about the world, and they can become a part of their belief system.

The Influence of Peers

As children grow, their peer groups become increasingly influential in shaping their attitudes and beliefs. Peer groups provide a social context where children learn to navigate social dynamics, including forming in-group and out-group distinctions. Peer pressure can play a significant role in the development of prejudiced attitudes. Children and adolescents may conform to the attitudes and behaviors of their peer groups to fit in or gain acceptance. If a peer group holds prejudiced views, individuals may adopt those views to maintain social bonds.

The development of prejudiced attitudes is not an isolated phenomenon but rather a product of socialization and exposure to stereotypes. Media, family, and peers all play significant roles in shaping these beliefs. Recognizing the influence of these agents of socialization is the first step in combatting prejudice and fostering a more inclusive and empathetic society.

Unmasking the Psychology of Hatred and Aggression

The complexities of human behavior and the spectrum of emotions that drive it have always been subjects of fascination, study, and exploration. One of the most perplexing and concerning aspects of human behavior is the capacity for hatred and aggression toward others. The roots of this behavior often lie deep within the psychological makeup of individuals, driven by a multitude of factors that propel them towards animosity and prejudice. Let us delve into the psychological factors that contribute to hatred and aggression, exploring how certain personality traits and psychological mechanisms can play a pivotal role in fostering animosity towards specific groups, such as international students.

However, before we embark, it's important to acknowledge a pivotal moment that led to the creation of this book. At a housewarming party-cum-religious function in Mississauga, I encountered an elderly individual whose beliefs and animosity towards international students from India were particularly toxic and unreasonable. As I wrote in the Introduction, this encounter left an indelible mark on me, serving as a catalyst for exploration into the depths of hatred and the quest to understand and address it. It became evident that this individual was not an isolated case, and there may be many more like him harboring similar sentiments that deserve illumination and transformation.

The Role of Psychological Factors

Psychological factors are instrumental in shaping our attitudes, beliefs, and behaviors. When it comes to hatred and aggression, certain psychological traits and mechanisms can significantly influence an individual's propensity to harbor animosity toward others. Here, we will delve into some of these influential factors.

Authoritarianism

One personality trait that can make individuals more prone to hatred and aggression is authoritarianism. An authoritarian individual tends to have a strong desire for order, control, and obedience to authority figures. They are often rigid in their thinking and can be intolerant of dissenting views or lifestyles that deviate from their own. In the context of international students, authoritarians may view them as disruptors of the established order or as a threat to societal norms. Their need for control and adherence to traditional values can lead to hostility towards those they perceive as challenging the status quo.

Low Empathy

Empathy, the ability to understand and share the feelings of others, is a critical factor in fostering compassion and reducing hatred. Individuals with low levels of empathy may struggle to connect with the experiences and struggles of others, making it easier for them to harbor negative attitudes and animosity. When it comes to international students, a lack of empathy can manifest itself as indifference or callousness towards the challenges they face. Those with low empathy may fail to recognize the hardships these students endure, leading to an unsympathetic and even hostile stance.

Scapegoating

Scapegoating is a psychological mechanism in which individuals or groups are unfairly blamed for problems or issues in society. It is a way of deflecting responsibility and attributing blame to a convenient target. Scapegoating often arises when individuals or communities face economic, social, or political challenges. In the context of international students, they may become convenient scapegoats for broader societal issues. When faced with economic downturns, unemployment, or cultural changes, some individuals may unjustly blame international students for these problems, fostering resentment and hostility.

Group Identity and Conformity – Us vs. Them

Human beings have a natural inclination to identify with social groups, whether based on nationality, religion, race, or other factors. This group identity can contribute to the 'us vs. them' mentality, where individuals develop a strong sense of loyalty and camaraderie with their in-group while viewing members of out-groups with suspicion or hostility. In the case of international students, this group identity dynamic can play out in various ways. Some individuals may perceive students as outsiders who don't share their values or cultural identity, leading to animosity. Conversely, international students themselves may form close-knit communities, potentially creating friction with the host community. It is common to see Tamil, Punjabi, or Gujarati students interacting within their language groups and not mixing around too much with members of other Indian communities even though English is a common language, and they all have to learn new ways of life and come to a new common ground. While Canada encourages multiculturalism, the melting pot theory comes into practice automatically in the modern world.

Fear and Threat Perception – The Dark Lens of Insecurity

Fear and threat perception are potent psychological drivers of hostility. When individuals perceive a threat to their well-being, whether real or imagined, it can trigger defensive reactions and a heightened sense of animosity towards the perceived threat. In the context of international students, the fear of economic competition, cultural change, or social disruption can contribute to the perception of these students as a threat. This fear can intensify feelings of hostility and prejudice as individuals seek to protect their perceived interests.

As we navigate the intricate landscape of human psychology, it becomes evident that hatred and aggression are not monolithic entities; instead, they are complex outcomes of various psychological factors. The last factor that I want to discuss is cognitive biases.

Cognitive Biases and their Impact on Inter-Community Relations

In our quest to understand the dynamics of division within immigrant communities, we must explore the profound influence of cognitive biases on our perceptions, beliefs, and attitudes towards out-groups. Cognitive biases are inherent shortcuts in our thinking processes, often leading us to make judgments and decisions that deviate from rationality and objectivity. They play a crucial role in shaping our perspectives and significantly affect our interactions with individuals from different backgrounds.

Confirmation bias is a cognitive bias that has far-reaching implications for how we process information and make sense of the world around us. It refers to our tendency to seek, interpret, and remember information in a way that confirms our pre-existing beliefs and values while ignoring or downplaying information that challenges them.

Consider this scenario: An individual, let's call him Veer, belongs to an immigrant community in Canada and holds certain beliefs about members of other immigrant communities. Veer believes that individuals from a particular community are more prone to criminal behavior. He avidly consumes media that perpetuates this stereotype, watching news reports and talk shows that disproportionately focus on crimes committed by members of this community. Veer's confirmation bias actively seeks out and amplifies information that aligns with his existing beliefs. Every news story that confirms his bias serves as a reinforcement of his convictions, leading to an increasingly more entrenched and polarised perspective.

In today's context, WhatsApp forwards serve as a significant amplifier of confirmation bias. Veer tends to share reports and messages that align with his negative perceptions of the community he dislikes. As he does so, he inadvertently reinforces his beliefs while conveniently overlooking similar messages related to members of his group or community. The same applies to the other forms of social media. There have been attempts to highlight these evils by movies like *The Hater*, which is a 2020 Polish film directed by Jan Komasa. The movie follows Tomasz, a young man who becomes embroiled in a world of online manipulation and political intrigue. Created by a talented team, including writer Mateusz Pacewicz and producer Krzysztof Rak, the film delves into the dark side of social media, exploring how it can be weaponized to manipulate public opinion and sow discord. Another movie that comes to mind is the Netflix documentary-drama titled *The Social Dilemma*. Also released in 2020, the film is directed by Jeff Orlowski and explores the impact of social media and technology on society. It features interviews with tech industry insiders, including former employees of major social media platforms, who discuss the addictive nature of these platforms, their influence on behavior, and the potential consequences for individuals and society.

As I listened to Punjabi media in Canada during my visit, I couldn't help but notice how confirmation bias played a significant role in the narratives being presented. The media sources often seemed to cherry-pick stories that reinforced the negative stereotypes associated with new immigrants. This selective reporting deepened the divide within the immigrant communities, perpetuating mistrust and animosity.

Understanding confirmation bias is essential because it provides insights into why individuals like Veer hold such rigid and often unfounded beliefs about out-groups. Recognizing this bias in ourselves and others can be the first step toward breaking down these barriers. It prompts us to question the sources of our information and encourages us to seek out diverse perspectives to gain a more comprehensive understanding of complex issues.

Another cognitive bias that significantly influences our perceptions of out-groups is the out-group homogeneity bias. This bias leads us to perceive members of an out-group as more similar to each other than they actually are while simultaneously recognizing the diversity within our group. We tend to paint members of other communities with a broad brush, assuming that they share the same characteristics, values, and behaviors.

Imagine a scenario where members of a particular immigrant community in Canada are viewed with suspicion and mistrust by another immigrant community. The out-group homogeneity bias may cause individuals from the second community to perceive all members of the first community as having similar customs, habits, and beliefs despite the rich diversity within the group. This oversimplification leads to a distorted view of the out-group, reinforcing stereotypes and fueling negative attitudes.

During my encounters with individuals holding animosity towards international students from India, I noticed the out-group homogeneity bias at play. Their unfavorable perceptions of students from India were often based on the actions of a few individuals or anecdotes they had heard, leading to a broad generalization that painted all international students from India with the same negative brush. This bias contributed to an unjust and unreasonable hostility.

Cognitive biases, such as confirmation bias and the out-group homogeneity bias, are not isolated phenomena but are interconnected and often mutually reinforcing. In the context of immigrant communities, these biases can lead to a vicious cycle of misunderstanding and mistrust.

Consider how confirmation bias and the out-group homogeneity bias can intersect. Veer's confirmation bias makes him more likely to accept and amplify negative stories about the out-group he mistrusts. Simultaneously, the out-group homogeneity bias may cause him to perceive all members of that out-group as sharing the same negative characteristics. This dual bias intensifies Veer's negative attitudes, making it even more challenging to bridge the gap between communities.

As we navigate the complexities of inter-community relations in Canada and beyond, it is essential to recognize the role of cognitive biases in perpetuating division. These biases are not insurmountable obstacles but rather cognitive tendencies that can be addressed through awareness and education.

By acknowledging the existence of these biases in ourselves and in society, we can take deliberate steps to counteract their influence and foster greater understanding and harmony among immigrant communities.

We need to delve deeper into strategies to mitigate the impact of cognitive biases, promote empathy and cross-cultural understanding, and ultimately work towards bridging the divides that exist within and between immigrant communities. I hope that by exploring these biases and their effects, we can pave the way for a more inclusive and interconnected society where diversity is celebrated and divisions are dismantled.

The Punjabi Language Media in Canada

In the diverse landscape of Canadian society, where immigrants from various backgrounds seek to build new lives, the media plays a pivotal role in shaping public perception, influencing attitudes, and fostering a sense of community. However, within the Punjabi language media in Canada, a concerning pattern has emerged, one that deserves scrutiny. It is a pattern that seems to selectively portray international students and recent immigrants in a negative light, perpetuating stereotypes and feeding into prejudiced attitudes.

For them, the earlier immigrants, the pioneers, are the heroes, and the new incumbents are the problem. This is, by and large, the opinion that I formed during my three months there in 2023 and a month that I spent there in 2015. It is not that they haven't ever highlighted the problems faced by the students. They sometimes engage in such practices, and on occasion, they feature stories of students who have performed remarkable acts of service. However, it seems to view the students as the out-group while positioning itself as part of the larger, already successful diaspora.

Canada has long been celebrated as a multicultural haven, a nation that prides itself on embracing diversity, welcoming immigrants, and fostering an inclusive society. This image of a melting pot of cultures, languages, and backgrounds has drawn people from around the world in search of a better life, including students pursuing higher education opportunities. However, the promise of inclusivity and equal opportunity doesn't always align with the portrayal of certain immigrant groups, particularly those in the Punjabi-speaking community, within the Punjabi language media in Canada.

While it is essential for media to report on all aspects of society, including the challenges faced by immigrants and students, a closer look at Indian language(s) media in Canada reveals a concerning bias. Yes, the media does report on crimes against students, but what stands out is its preference for stories where a student is involved in committing a crime, no matter how petty or even when they are merely accused of wrongdoing. This selective reporting not only creates a skewed image but also perpetuates negative stereotypes about international students and recent immigrants.

One of the most troubling aspects of this media bias is the sensationalism of petty crimes committed by students. While it is essential to report on criminal activities, the disproportionate focus on minor offenses by international students serves to exaggerate their significance. This skewed narrative can lead to the perception that students are disproportionately involved in criminal behavior, which is both inaccurate and unfair.

Additionally, the use of derogatory language and a judgmental tone in YouTube talk shows further compounds the issue. Instead of fostering understanding and empathy, such language perpetuates stereotypes, reinforces biases, and, at times, even dehumanizes students and recent immigrants.

Another disconcerting trend within Punjabi language media in Canada is the intrusive coverage of young students' personal lives. Love affairs and live-in relationships are presented as if they were grave crimes of moral transgressions. This type of coverage not only invades the privacy of individuals but also contributes to a culture of shaming and judgment.

Young students, like anyone else, should have the right to personal choices and privacy without being subjected to public scrutiny and judgment. Such media practices not only perpetuate negative stereotypes but also discourage open conversations about healthy relationships and personal choices.

The Role of Socialization and Stereotyping

To understand why Punjabi language media in Canada may engage in such selective and biased reporting, it is crucial to examine the role of socialization and the power of stereotypes. The media, in particular, holds immense power as an agent of socialization. It shapes our understanding of the world, influences our perceptions, and helps construct our cultural norms and values. Media messages, whether explicit or subtle, can reinforce existing beliefs and stereotypes or challenge them. In the context of Punjabi language media in Canada, the portrayal of international students and recent immigrants can be seen as a reflection of broader societal attitudes and biases.

When the media consistently portrays certain groups, such as international students, in a negative light, it reinforces these stereotypes and contributes to the development of prejudiced attitudes among the audience. For example, when the media disproportionately highlights the involvement of international students in petty crimes, it fosters the stereotype that they are prone to criminal behavior. Likewise, when talk shows use derogatory language and judgemental tones towards students and recent immigrants, it deepens the belief that these individuals are deserving of scorn or suspicion.

Media holds a significant responsibility in shaping public opinion and influencing societal attitudes. While recognizing this, it is essential for Punjabi language media in Canada, like all media outlets, to commit to ethical reporting that promotes fairness, accuracy, and inclusivity.

Instead of perpetuating stereotypes and focusing on sensationalism, the media can choose to highlight the positive contributions of international students and recent immigrants to Canadian society. They can also foster an environment of understanding and empathy by addressing the challenges these individuals face, such as adapting to a new culture, navigating the education system, acquiring extra skills, or finding employment.

Instead, the talk shows on YouTube have become the battlegrounds where these issues are debated, and opinions are shouted louder than facts.

Gurpreet

At the heart of this media frenzy was Gurpreet (name changed), a young student from Punjab who had recently moved to Canada for his higher education. He had always been a keen observer of the world around him, and it didn't take long for him to become immersed in the discourse of Punjabi media.

One evening, as Gurpreet scrolled through his YouTube feed, he stumbled upon a talk show on the problems faced by the immigrants. The show featured a panel of opinionated individuals, but one voice stood out amongst the rest – a lady who repeatedly proclaimed that Canada should halt the spouse visa programs, preventing husbands and wives from living together on Canadian soil.

Gurpreet was astounded by the audacity of such a suggestion. The lady argued vehemently, claiming that many immigrants were taking advantage of this visa program, leading to family disintegration and moral decay. Her words were sharp and unyielding, and she painted a bleak picture of the Punjabi community in Canada.

As the show progressed, Gurpreet couldn't help but notice how personal anecdotes were elevated to universal truths, and petty crimes by a few students were blown out of proportion to reflect negatively on the entire community. The lady on the panel was joined by others who criticized everything from the existence of 'IELTS shops' to allegations of examiners being lenient. 'IELTS shops' was a derogatory term used to describe the IELTS training institutes that dotted the landscape of Punjab. These institutes claimed to train students to improve their English skills to ace the IELTS exams, a crucial step for many international students aspiring to study in Canada. While it was true that some of these institutes were substandard and operated with questionable ethics, Gurpreet knew that students were not to be blamed for that. They were victims themselves, investing their parents' hard-earned money in the hopes of a brighter future for their children. The institute owners were unscrupulous in that they employed cheap, underqualified, and underpaid teachers who could not help these children improve their language.

The allegations against IELTS examiners were particularly concerning. Instead of recognizing the rigorous testing process, the talk show participants claimed that examiners were influenced and lenient towards certain candidates, especially those from Punjab. This baseless accusation put immense pressure on the examiners, leading them to be overly cautious and stringent in their evaluations.

Gurpreet, an aspiring writer himself, couldn't remain silent any longer. He felt compelled to speak out against these injustices, to present the other side of the story. With a sense of purpose burning within him, he decided to call into one of the talk shows, hoping to shed light on the truth.

The evening of the talk show appearance arrived, and Gurpreet found himself nervously sitting in front of his computer, dialing into the show. The host, a charismatic but confrontational figure, introduced him as a 'concerned student' and allowed him to speak. 'I agree that there are issues with some IELTS institutes,' Gurpreet began, his voice shaking slightly with nervousness. 'But it's important to remember that many students are sincere in their efforts to improve their English. They pay their hard-earned money for coaching, and it's not their fault if the quality is subpar.'

He continued, 'As for the allegations against examiners, it's quite the opposite. They face immense pressure and scrutiny due to these accusations, and they often end up giving lower scores than the applicants deserve just to safeguard their jobs. It's not fair as the student stands to lose marks, opportunities, and money.'

The response from the talk show panel was immediate and harsh. One panelist accused Gurpreet of being naive and unaware of the ground realities. Other panelists chimed in, dismissing his points as misguided and irrelevant.

Gurpreet felt a sense of frustration building within him. He had hoped for a constructive dialogue, but instead, he was met with hostility and mockery. The talk show had become a platform where sensationalism and shouting down opposing views prevailed over genuine discourse.

As the show concluded, Gurpreet couldn't help but feel disillusioned. He wanted to present a balanced perspective to shed light on the complexities of the issues discussed. Instead, he had been bullied and silenced, his concerns brushed aside. In the days that followed, Gurpreet reflected on his experience. He realized that the problems within the Punjabi community in Canada were not limited to the issues discussed on talk shows. It was the toxic environment of sensationalism, judgment, and moral policing that was tearing the community apart.

Gurpreet was determined not to be discouraged by his initial setback. He knew that change would not come overnight, but he also knew that it was essential to continue speaking out against injustice and misinformation. Someone told him about me and my intention of writing a book on the subject. He arranged for us to meet at a coffee shop and discuss his experience. The road ahead was challenging, but Gurpreet had learned that silence was not an option. He was determined to be a voice of reason and compassion in the cacophonous world of Punjabi media in Canada, where sensationalism and blame had taken precedence over understanding and unity. Even though busy with his studies, he has decided to start a podcast that gives the other point of view and is more accommodating. He asked me if I would join him in his endeavor, to which I assured him that I would make every effort to help.

Simran

Around the same time, I heard of an incident that took place in 2021. In the heart of a bustling Punjabi student community in Canada lived a young woman named Simran (name changed). She was a diligent student who had moved to Canada with dreams of a bright future. Simran had always been focused on her studies, working tirelessly towards her goal of becoming a pharmacist. However, even the most diligent students sometimes yearn for a break, a moment to let loose and unwind.

One Friday evening, after a particularly grueling week of juggling work, studies, and the pressures of being a responsible adult far from home, Simran decided it was time to let her hair down. She had never been much of a drinker, having grown up in a conservative family in Punjab, but the temptation to experience student life in Canada finally got the better of her.

Simran invited a few close friends over to her modest apartment. Sharing stories and laughter, she decided to try alcohol for the first time, getting intoxicated. A friend recorded a short video of her holding a drink, her cheeks flushed with the excitement of trying something new, stumbling slightly as she sang a Punjabi song. Little did Simran know that this video would soon kick up a storm.

The following Monday, as Simran walked through the university campus, her phone buzzed incessantly with notifications. She was puzzled until she checked her social media accounts and saw her face, holding a drink, plastered across YouTube. The video had gone viral, and the caption read, 'Punjabi Student's Wild Night Out!'

Simran's heart sank as she read the comments below the video. People were quick to judge, labeling her as irresponsible and a disgrace to the community. They were making assumptions about her entire life based on a single moment captured on video. She felt humiliated, but she was also determined not to let this incident define her. Simran had bigger dreams, and she knew that she couldn't allow the judgments of others to derail her path.

As the days passed, the YouTubers, who often posed as the self-appointed moral police for the Punjabi community in Canada, refused to let the video fade into obscurity. They saw it as an opportunity to play judge and jury, repeatedly posting and commenting on Simran's video as if it were the embodiment of the entire Punjabi student community's behavior. I heard that she was a topic of conversation on an Indian-language radio channel, and it's not challenging to speculate on the content of their discussion about her.

Simran's close friends rallied around her, offering support and encouragement. They reminded her of her resilience and determination, urging her not to let the judgment of others shake her confidence. But it was Simran herself who found the strength within to rise above the negativity.

Despite the online vitriol, Simran continued to focus on her studies and her job. She worked night shifts as a security guard to make ends meet, even as she was bombarded with comments suggesting she was unfit for such a role. It was not an easy job, but she remained undeterred.

Simran knew that the upcoming pharmacy exams were crucial to her future, and she could not afford to let the incident affect her performance. She dedicated every spare moment to her studies, determined to prove to herself and her family that she could achieve her dreams.

Months passed, and Simran's dedication paid off. She passed her pharmacy exams with flying colors, earning the respect and admiration of her professors and colleagues. It was a sweet victory, and Simran knew that it was a testament to her strength and resilience. Despite the ongoing scrutiny from the online community, Simran secured a job in a reputable pharmacy. She refused to let the incident define her, and she was determined to make the most of her opportunity.

One day, she received a message from a fellow student who had watched her journey from the sidelines. The message read, 'You inspire me, Simran. Despite all the judgment and negativity, you never gave up on your dreams. You proved that the judgments made by others don't define one's true identity. Thank you for showing us all what true resilience looks like.'

Simran smiled as she read the message. She knew that she had emerged from the storm stronger than ever, and she hoped that her story would serve as a reminder to others that they, too, could overcome the harshest judgments and pursue their dreams with unwavering determination.

The Allure of Negativity and Its Impact

In an age when information flows ceaselessly from screens and speakers, it is no secret that the media, the world over, has an insatiable appetite for negativity. The reasons behind this phenomenon are complex, but the consequences are all too real.

Negativity, it seems, has become the lifeblood of modern media. Whether it is newspapers, television, radio, or the ever-expanding universe of the Internet, stories that spark outrage, fear, or controversy hold a magnetic pull on audiences. Such stories draw more eyeballs, more clicks, and more ears, and in the world of media, attention equals revenue.

One need not look far to find examples of this propensity for negativity. Newspapers splash sensational headlines across their front pages, often focussing on crime, scandal, or tragedy. Television news broadcasts dedicate significant airtime to stories that can incite fear or anger, while radio talk shows thrive on heated debates and confrontations. Online platforms, with their infinite space for content, sometimes descend into echo chambers of outrage and hostility.

But why does the media gravitate toward negativity with such enthusiasm? Part of the answer lies in human psychology. Studies have shown that negative information, such as threats or dangers, tends to grab our attention more effectively than positive information. It is an evolutionary trait, a survival mechanism that has been hardwired into our brains over millennia.

Media organizations, keenly aware of this psychological phenomenon, exploit it to their advantage. Stories of conflict, scandal, and catastrophe trigger a surge of emotions within audiences, ensuring that they remain glued to their screens. As long as the viewership numbers stay high, advertisers continue to pay top dollar for advertising slots, ensuring the media's financial health. However, the consequences of this relentless focus on negativity are far-reaching. It has a profound impact on the collective psyche of society. People consume a steady diet of distressing news, sensationalized reports, and doom-laden narratives, all of which leave an indelible mark on their minds.

Individuals who absorb this constant stream of negativity often find themselves living in a perpetual state of anxiety and fear. They grow wary of the world around them, perpetually on edge, and mistrustful of others. The stories they encounter convince them that danger lurks around every corner, and they become increasingly isolated, retreating into the safety of their bubbles. Families are torn apart by heated arguments over political issues fuelled by divisive media narratives. Friendships crumble under the weight of differing opinions and emotional fatigue. And in extreme cases, individuals fall into a state of despair, overwhelmed by a constant barrage of bad news.

Take, for example, the case of Ravi, a young Punjabi student who had recently arrived in Canada. Excited and hopeful about his future, he had been captivated by the allure of negativity perpetuated by the media. Night after night, he watched news reports that highlighted incidents of hate crimes and discrimination against immigrants. The constant exposure to such stories weighed heavily on Ravi's mind. He became consumed by fear and apprehension, believing that the world outside was a hostile and unwelcoming place. These negative narratives began to color his interactions with others, making it difficult for him to trust anyone beyond his small circle of friends.

It wasn't long before Ravi's mental health began to suffer. His anxiety levels soared, and he found it increasingly challenging to focus on his studies and adapt to his new environment. The relentless negativity of the media had cast a shadow over his aspirations, making it difficult for him to see the opportunities that lay ahead. As Ravi's story illustrates, the impact of media negativity can be profound and lasting. It has the power to shape individuals' worldviews, influence their beliefs and behaviors, and ultimately affect their well-being. Recognizing this, media organizations must take responsibility for the stories they tell and their potential consequences.

Media outlets, whatever the medium, have a unique role to play in society. They are not merely purveyors of information but also shapers of public perception. They have the power to choose which stories to emphasize and how to frame them. With that power comes a moral obligation to balance the scales, to report not only on the problems and challenges but also on the solutions and triumphs that define the human experience.

Responsible media can still draw attention, but it can do so by highlighting stories of resilience, compassion, and progress. It can showcase the contributions of immigrants and the positive impact they had on their adopted communities. It can provide a platform for voices that advocate for unity, understanding, and dialogue rather than division and hostility.

Moreover, media outlets need to recognize that newly arrived students like Ravi might become their clientele in the future.

These young individuals represent not only an audience but also a potential source of growth and prosperity. By nurturing their well-being and fostering a sense of belonging, the media can build lasting relationships with them.

In a rapidly changing world, the media can play a pivotal role in shaping the narrative of the Punjabi student community in Canada. By focusing on the positive contributions and success stories of its members, the media can help dispel stereotypes and create a more inclusive and welcoming environment.

As Ravi slowly began to distance himself from the constant stream of negative news and sought out more balanced sources of information, he discovered a community of like-minded individuals who were determined to build bridges, not walls. Through their support and encouragement, he is slowly regaining his confidence and optimism.

The media has the power to uplift and inspire, to foster a sense of unity and shared purpose. It is a responsibility that should not be taken lightly. As the Punjabi student community in Canada continues to grow and evolve, the media has an opportunity to be a force for positive change, guiding individuals like Ravi toward a brighter and more hopeful future.

I would be especially delighted if Hindi or Punjabi channels in Canada view this critique as an opportunity for constructive change. It is my sincere hope that they might consider reaching out and inviting me to collaborate on initiatives aimed at fostering productive dialogues and informative shows. These platforms can serve as spaces where both the older and newer generations of migrants can gain insights into the consequences of alienating one another and how to work together to forge connections that will contribute to the community's future well-being.

By engaging in open discussions, we can dispel the notion that dismissing one generation in favor of the other is a viable solution. Instead, we can emphasize the importance of mutual understanding and cooperation. These initiatives can showcase the richness of intergenerational perspectives, emphasising the strengths and experiences that each group brings to the table.

Through meaningful conversations and informative programming, we can bridge the generational gap that sometimes exists within immigrant communities. More importantly, we can impress on them that it is merely a generational gap and that the problems the elders find among the newcomers exist in all communities and not just their community. The goal is to create synergies that will not only benefit the present generation but also lay a foundation for a thriving and harmonious future. Together, we can work toward a shared vision of unity and collaboration, demonstrating that when generations come together with respect and empathy, they have the power to overcome challenges and build a stronger, more vibrant community.

In an ideal world, it is crucial for society to recognize the power of media and to engage in critical thinking when consuming news and information. By being discerning consumers of media content and advocating for ethical reporting, we can collectively work towards a more inclusive and empathetic society where individuals are not unfairly judged based on stereotypes and selective reporting. Unfortunately, it's not an ideal world, is it?

Navigating the Modern Canadian Immigration Maze

Comfortable in their own truths, the elders think the present generation just walks into Canada as and when it pleases them. Nothing could be further from the truth. Contrary to the common perception held by many from the older generation, immigrating to Canada is far from an easy feat. Gone are the days when one could simply pack their bags and make their way to the land of maple leaves with minimal effort. Today, the Canadian immigration process is characterized by a complex web of regulations, multiple layers of steps, rigorous checks, and stringent balances.

Back in the 1970s, Canada was a different country, and the immigration landscape was a world apart from what it is today. For many immigrants, especially those from Commonwealth countries like India, entering Canada was almost as simple as catching a flight. These newcomers didn't require a visa and often chose unconventional routes. A common strategy was to travel to Germany and then hop on a flight to Canada, arriving with dreams of securing work at farms and lumber mills. The process was spontaneous, and the paperwork was minimal.

Fast forward to the present, and the panorama has shifted dramatically. The immigration process to Canada now operates under a sophisticated and well-structured system. The beliefs held by some from the older generation, steeped in nostalgia, often display a stark ignorance of the complexities and stringent requirements of the current immigration processes. The dream of Canada endures, but it has evolved. It remains a land of opportunity, but the journey to reach it has become more demanding. To those who aspire to make Canada their home, you must remember that the path may be challenging, but the destination is worth the effort. The maple leaf still beckons, but it now flutters amid the intricate threads of a carefully woven tapestry—one that welcomes those who bring value, commitment, and a willingness to embrace the complexity of the Canadian immigration experience.

The Evolution of Canadian Immigration

Canada has long been known as a country that values immigration and diversity. Historically, the nation welcomed newcomers with open arms, particularly during the post-World War II era. In the 1970s, the Canadian government operated under a more relaxed immigration policy. It was a time when the term 'visa' held little significance for many hopeful migrants.

Back then, coming from a Commonwealth country like India had its perks. There was a certain sense of familiarity and camaraderie that existed between Canada and its Commonwealth counterparts. It was this friendly relationship that facilitated the entry of immigrants. People would often embark on journeys to Canada with little more than dreams and determination. They'd arrive, explore opportunities, and establish themselves.

In those days, the Canadian immigration system didn't demand extensive paperwork, complex application processes, or stringent qualifications. It was a different era, and immigrants enjoyed a more straightforward path to settling in Canada.

Today, the landscape has changed dramatically. The immigration process in Canada is governed by a meticulously designed framework that decades of policy evolution, societal changes, and global dynamics have shaped. Contrary to the beliefs of some, immigrating to Canada in the twenty-first century is not for the faint-hearted.

Today, Canada offers several immigration programs and schemes to cater to a wide range of individuals, including those seeking permanent residence, temporary work, and family reunification. Discussed here are some of the notable immigration schemes and programs. I have included the Labor Market Impact Assessment (LMIA) as one of the immigration pathways.

Express Entry System

This is Canada's primary system for managing applications for permanent residence under federal economic immigration programs. It includes the Federal Skilled Worker Program (FSWP), the Federal Skilled Trades Program (FSTP), and the Canadian Experience Class (CEC).

The Express Entry system lies at the heart of the modern Canadian immigration system. It is a points-based system designed to select candidates who are most likely to contribute to the Canadian economy. Applicants are evaluated based on factors such as age, education, work experience, language proficiency, and more. The Comprehensive Ranking System (CRS) assigns scores to candidates, and only those with high scores receive an Invitation to Apply (ITA) for permanent residence.

To say that getting into the Express Entry pool is competitive would be an understatement. Aspirants need to have exceptional credentials to stand a chance. This system is a far cry from the spontaneous journeys of the 1970s.

Provincial Nominee Program (PNP)

In addition to the federal Express Entry system, Canada's provinces and territories (except for Quebec) have their own immigration programs known as the Provincial Nominee Programs (PNPs). These programs allow regions to nominate candidates for permanent residence based on their specific economic and labor market needs. Applicants must meet the unique criteria of each PNP, adding further complexity to the whole process.

Family Sponsorship

Canadian citizens and permanent residents can sponsor their close family members, such as spouses, parents, grandparents, dependent children, and adopted children, to become permanent residents. Family reunification and humanitarian considerations remain integral aspects of Canadian immigration.

However, even these categories are subject to thorough vetting and strict regulations. Family sponsors must meet financial requirements, and applicants seeking humanitarian and compassionate grounds must provide compelling evidence to support their claims.

Refugee and Asylum Programs

Canada offers protection to refugees through various programs, including the Refugee and Humanitarian Resettlement Program and the In-Canada Asylum Program.

Quebec Immigration Programs

The province of Quebec has its own immigration programs, including the Quebec Skilled Worker Program (QSWP) and the Quebec Experience Program (PEQ), designed to attract skilled workers and graduates to the province.

Atlantic Immigration Pilot Program (AIPP)

This program facilitates the immigration of skilled workers and international graduates to Canada's Atlantic provinces: New Brunswick, Newfoundland and Labrador, Nova Scotia, and Prince Edward Island.

Start-up Visa Program

This program is designed to attract innovative entrepreneurs with viable business ideas to establish and operate businesses in Canada.

Rural and Northern Immigration Pilot (RNIP)

The RNIP allows participating communities in rural and northern regions of Canada to recommend foreign workers for permanent residence, addressing local labor market needs.

Caregiver Program

This program enables qualified individuals to work as caregivers for children, the elderly, or people with high medical needs in Canada, leading to permanent residence.

Self-employed Persons Program

This program is for individuals who have the intention and ability to become self-employed in Canada in cultural or athletic activities or farming.

International Mobility Program (IMP)

The IMP allows the entry of foreign workers without the need for a Labor Market Impact Assessment (LMIA) under certain categories, including working holiday programs, reciprocal agreements, and more.

Temporary Foreign Worker Program (TFWP)

Employers can hire foreign workers for specific jobs through the TFWP, typically by obtaining an LMIA.

LMIA-Based Work Permits

This category allows foreign workers to obtain work permits in Canada when employers have obtained a Labor Market Impact Assessment (LMIA) to demonstrate that there are no qualified Canadians or permanent residents available for the job beyond a certain percentage, and that percentage is decided and reviewed by the government from time to time.

Study Permits

International students can come to Canada by obtaining a study permit. Some graduates may be eligible for post-graduation work permits and pathways to permanent residence.

Humanitarian and Compassionate (H&C) Applications

People in Canada with exceptional circumstances may apply for permanent residence on humanitarian and compassionate grounds, even if they don't meet typical immigration requirements.

At the end of this book, I have placed a description of the steps involved for some of the above entries and the complexities involved, listing the process that an aspirant needs to follow.

One of the most persistent myths among the older generation is the belief that immigrants from Commonwealth countries like India still find it easy to enter Canada. This misconception can lead to significant disappointment and confusion. While it is true that some Commonwealth citizens may still enjoy certain visa exemptions for short visits, the ability to stay in Canada for an extended period, work, or seek permanent residence involves a far more elaborate process. The days of catching a flight to Canada with minimal documentation are long gone.

The Reality of Today's Immigration

In the modern era, the Canadian immigration process has transformed into a complex and highly regulated system. Aspirants must embark on a journey that demands meticulous planning, comprehensive documentation, and a thorough understanding of the stringent criteria that govern the process.

The contemporary Canadian immigration landscape resembles a labyrinth, with multiple paths and programs, each tailored to specific objectives and criteria. Understanding this system is paramount for anyone seeking to make Canada their new home. Whether it's permanent residence, temporary work permits, or international studies, the requirements are comprehensive, and compliance is non-negotiable.

Canada is seen, especially in India, as a land of opportunity, a nation celebrated for its inclusivity, diversity, and social welfare systems. Yet, this opportunity comes with a price, one that demands careful preparation, unwavering dedication, and an unyielding commitment to meeting the strict standards outlined by the Canadian government.

Meticulous Planning

Prospective immigrants must engage in meticulous planning to navigate the Canadian immigration system successfully. They should assess their eligibility, understand the specific requirements of their chosen immigration pathway, and develop a comprehensive strategy for the journey ahead.

One crucial aspect of this planning involves determining the most suitable immigration program. Is Express Entry the right fit, or would a Provincial Nominee Program better align with an individual's qualifications and aspirations? These decisions require thoughtful consideration and often necessitate consultation with immigration experts or legal professionals.

Comprehensive Documentation

The significance of comprehensive documentation in the immigration process cannot be overstated. Applicants must compile and submit an extensive array of documents, ranging from educational transcripts and work experience certificates to language proficiency test results and police clearance certificates. Each document must adhere to specific guidelines, and any oversight can result in delays or even rejection.

The accuracy of the information provided is of utmost importance. Any inconsistencies or inaccuracies will raise red flags and lead to adverse outcomes. Therefore, meticulous attention to detail in assembling and verifying documentation is essential.

What many might not realize is that the process goes beyond just providing documents; it involves rigorous verification by third-party entities chosen by the Canadian authorities but paid for by the prospective immigrant or student. One prominent example of such a third-party entity is the World Education Services (WES), which evaluates educational qualifications.

The Canadian government places a high premium on the authenticity of documents provided by applicants. They understand that the accuracy of information is crucial for preserving the integrity of the immigration system and ensuring that only qualified individuals are granted entry.

To achieve this, third-party entities are employed to verify critical components of an applicant's profile. These entities are independent organizations with expertise in assessing specific types of documents or qualifications. They play a pivotal role in determining the legitimacy of an applicant's claims.

One of the most critical aspects of the immigration process is the verification of educational qualifications. Canada, like many countries, values education and places great importance on the educational backgrounds of immigrants. As a result, educational documents, such as degrees, diplomas, and transcripts, undergo rigorous scrutiny.

WES evaluates foreign educational credentials to determine their equivalence in the Canadian education system. This evaluation is crucial for assessing an applicant's eligibility for immigration programs that have educational requirements. Applicants are required to submit their educational documents to WES, which then assesses the authenticity of the documents and compares them to Canadian educational standards. This evaluation helps Canadian immigration authorities determine whether an applicant's educational background aligns with the criteria for their chosen immigration program.

In addition to educational qualifications, language proficiency is another critical aspect of Canadian immigration. Applicants are required to demonstrate their proficiency in either English or French, Canada's official languages. Third-party language testing organizations, such as the International English Language

Testing System (IELTS) and the Test d'évaluation de français (TEF), play an essential role in assessing and verifying language skills of applicants.

Moreover, various other aspects of an applicant's profile may undergo third-party verification. For example, work experience may be evaluated by professional organizations or industry-specific bodies to ensure its accuracy and authenticity. Police clearance certificates, which are often required to demonstrate good character and a clean criminal record, are issued by law enforcement agencies and may be subject to verification.

The Consequences of Inaccuracies

The consequences of providing inaccurate or inconsistent information during the immigration process can be severe. The Canadian government places a high degree of trust in the information provided by applicants, and any breach of that trust can result in adverse outcomes.

Inaccurate information can lead to delays in processing, requests for additional documentation, or, in some cases, outright rejection of the application. In cases of intentional misrepresentation or fraud, applicants may face serious consequences, including bans on future applications and potential removal from Canada if they are already in the country.

Furthermore, inconsistencies or inaccuracies can damage an applicant's credibility, making it challenging to rebuild trust with Canadian immigration authorities. This underscores the importance of meticulous attention to detail and the verification of all the information and documents before submission.

The Prospective Immigrant's Responsibility

While third-party entities play a significant role in document verification, the responsibility for providing accurate and authentic information rests solely with the prospective immigrant or student. It is incumbent upon them to ensure that all the documents and information submitted are truthful and verifiable. While it is clear now in the contemporary Canadian immigration landscape that the accuracy and authenticity of information are non-negotiable, I have often heard the elders say that these kids are coming on fake certificates and degrees. A case did happen where students from Punjab were given fake offer letters to colleges and courses in Canada. It must be pointed out that those students did not furnish any false documents and were, in fact, victims of fraud where unscrupulous agents cheated them. The elders often cite this case as if it were the fault of the students who stare at an uncertain future, even as I write this book.

Third-party entities like WES and language testing organizations play a crucial role in verifying the claims made by applicants. Inaccuracies or inconsistencies can lead to delays, rejections, or even serious consequences. Therefore, prospective immigrants and students must approach the immigration process with meticulous attention to detail and a commitment to providing truthful and verifiable information. By doing so, they not only enhance their chances of success but also uphold the integrity of the Canadian immigration system.

In the contemporary Canadian immigration landscape, eligibility criteria are rigorous. Meeting these criteria necessitates not only educational and professional qualifications but also adaptability and the ability to demonstrate one's value to Canada. The government seeks individuals who can contribute to the country's economy, society, or culture in meaningful ways.

For instance, the Express Entry system rewards youth, higher education, and skilled work experience. Proficiency in one of Canada's official languages—English or French—is another crucial factor. Provincial Nominee Programs, on the other hand, may prioritize candidates who possess qualifications or experience in specific industries or occupations needed within that province.

The path to Canada is not a linear journey. It is often fraught with challenges, uncertainties, and setbacks. Persistence and adaptability are essential qualities that prospective immigrants must cultivate. The process may include re-evaluating eligibility, improving language skills, gaining additional work experience, or even revisiting the choice of immigration pathway.

Applicants must also prepare for a period of waiting, as processing times can vary significantly based on numerous factors, including the specific immigration program and the volume of applications being processed.

The point remains that complexities and an evolving set of requirements now mark the journey to Canada. While the path may be demanding, the younger generation thinks that the destination—the promise of a brighter future in a diverse, prosperous, and inclusive nation—is worth the effort. This clearly arises from a contrast between the opportunities available in their home country and the possibilities presented by the new one.

The Dark Side of Immigration: LMIA and Refugee Programs

It is common knowledge that many immigrants do not meet the stringent requirements listed above. They, therefore, resort to other means and either seek employment through the LMIA programs mentioned at the beginning of the chapter or the loopholes in the Refugee and Asylum Programs.

Canada's Labor Market Impact Assessment (LMIA) program is designed to help Canadian employers fill specific job positions with foreign workers when there are no qualified Canadians or permanent residents available for the job. It's a mechanism to ensure that Canadian businesses can access the talent they need to thrive. However, within this system, there lurk unscrupulous elements, some of whom are Canadian citizens themselves, primarily of Indian origin, exploiting the dreams of aspiring immigrants.

To understand how this exploitation unfolds, let's first look at the basics of the LMIA process. Canadian employers seeking to hire foreign workers must apply for an LMIA from the government. This application involves demonstrating the genuine need for the foreign worker and meeting various criteria. The government assesses the application to ensure that the employment of a foreign worker will not negatively impact the Canadian labor market.

In the LMIA pathway, certain business owners, many of them from the Indian community, exploit their fellow countrymen who aspire to make Canada their new home. These established Canadian business owners indeed need the manpower to fuel their enterprises, and they seek LMIAs to hire foreign workers. However, they turn this need into a money-making opportunity.

The alleged modus operandi of these unscrupulous business owners is to offer LMIAs to aspiring immigrants but at a steep price. This practice is unethical and preys on the hopes and dreams of individuals who are seeking a better life in Canada. To be clear, not all established Indian businessmen engage in this unethical practice, but a significant number do.

The businessmen in this scenario are obviously individuals who are not new immigrants or students but are, instead, already established Canadian citizens. They have successfully obtained Canadian citizenship and are now exploiting their fellow countrymen. They are part of the same group that sometimes criticizes and denigrates the current generation of immigrants.

The exorbitant fees charged by these unscrupulous business owners are allegedly staggering. It is suspected that aspiring immigrants pay anywhere between 25,000 and 50,000 Canadian dollars for these LMIA opportunities. This is a significant financial burden, especially for individuals who are already investing heavily in their Canadian dream. These funds could be better spent on settlement and integration, education, or other essential expenses.

The Canadian government faces a big dilemma in this situation. While it can verify the genuine need for foreign workers and ensure that candidates possess the required skills and experience, it cannot prevent unethical businesses from exploiting the system. The government's role is primarily to uphold the integrity of the immigration process, but it cannot control the actions of private individuals.

The Refugee Status Scam: A Web of Deception

The refugee status pathway is another avenue where, it is alleged, the exploitation of aspiring immigrants occurs. In this scheme, certain organizations, often referred to as 'separatist' groups, allegedly capitalize on the aspirations of individuals by claiming they are persecuted in their home country.

To better understand this scam, let's delve into the refugee process in Canada. To qualify for refugee status, individuals must demonstrate that they face persecution, torture, or risk to their life or freedom in their home country due to race, religion, nationality, political opinion, or membership in a particular social group. Certain separatist organizations, both in Canada and India, are alleged to play a significant role in this exploitation. These organizations provide memberships to aspiring immigrants, often charging hefty fees for these memberships. Once individuals become members, these organizations certify them as part of a persecuted group, claiming that they are at risk in their home country.

The refugee status pathway has become a lucrative market for these organizations. They sell membership letters to aspiring immigrants for substantial sums. Allegations abound that extra charges are levied for photographs and selfies with the leaders of these groups. The applicants are led to believe that such photographs strengthen their case, even though this is not a legitimate part of the refugee claim process.

This exploitation not only undermines the integrity of the Canadian immigration system but also preys upon the desperation and vulnerability of individuals seeking refuge and a better life. It tarnishes the reputation of those who genuinely need asylum and puts their claims at risk.

As far as the Canadian government is concerned, its policy is based on genuinely helping refugees. It's important to note that the eligibility criteria, application processes, and timelines for the settlement of refugees can vary depending on the specific refugee category and program.

The Canadian government continually reviews and updates its refugee and immigration policies, but broadly speaking, in Canada, refugees can obtain permanent residence rights through various immigration programs, with one of the primary pathways being the Refugee and Humanitarian Resettlement Program. To be considered a refugee and qualify for permanent residence, individuals must meet specific criteria outlined in the Immigration and Refugee Protection Act (IRPA) and be recognized as refugees by the Canadian government. Here's an overview of the process.

Refugee Status Determination (RSD)

To be considered a refugee in Canada, a person must demonstrate a well-founded fear of persecution or risk of serious harm if they return to their home country. This fear can be based on various factors, such as race, religion, nationality, political opinion, or membership in a particular social group. Refugees can apply for recognition through one of the following avenues:

In-Canada Refugee Claim

Individuals who arrive in Canada and make a refugee claim at a port of entry or at a designated inland office may have their case heard by the Immigration and Refugee Board of Canada (IRB).

If the IRB determines that they meet the refugee definition, they may be granted refugee status.

Referral by the UNHCR

Some refugees are referred to Canada for resettlement by the United Nations High Commissioner for Refugees (UNHCR). These individuals are pre-screened by the UNHCR, and Canada reviews their case for potential resettlement.

Refugee Sponsorship

Once a person is recognized as a refugee, they may become eligible for permanent residence through one of the following sponsorship programs:

Government-Assisted Refugees (GAR)

The Canadian government sponsors these refugees. The government provides financial and settlement support to GARs for their first year in Canada.

Privately Sponsored Refugees (PSR)

Private individuals, groups, or organizations can sponsor refugees to come to Canada. These sponsors commit to providing financial and settlement support to the sponsored refugees.

Blended Visa Office-Referred (BVOR) Program

This program combines government assistance and private sponsorship for refugees. The government covers a portion of the resettlement costs, and private sponsors contribute the rest.

Family Reunification

If a refugee has family members who are also refugees or have received permanent residence in Canada, they may be eligible for family reunification.

Resettlement

Some refugees may be eligible for resettlement programs in

Canada, such as the Resettlement Assistance Program (RAP), which provides immediate financial support and settlement services to help them integrate into Canadian society. The definition of who qualifies as a refugee in Canada is based on international agreements, primarily the 1951 United Nations Convention Relating to the Status of Refugees and its 1967 Protocol. Refugees are individuals who meet the criteria defined in these agreements and who have a well-founded fear of persecution or serious harm in their home country based on specific grounds. These grounds typically include race, religion, nationality, political opinion, and membership in a particular social group.

The Paradox of Exploitation

We have seen the disheartening reality of exploitation within the Canadian immigration system by members of the same community as the ones exploited. A particularly poignant aspect of this exploitation is that those who perpetrate it are often well-established, affluent individuals who have called Canada home for decades. Not only do they allegedly charge exorbitant amounts to aspiring immigrants, but they also sit in judgment of them, often denouncing newcomers with derogatory labels such as 'uncouth' and 'ill-mannered'. This paradox underscores the complexity of human behavior.

One of the most troubling aspects of this exploitation is that it occurs within the same community. Individuals who have successfully navigated the challenges of immigration settled into their new lives, and often achieved financial success choose to exploit their fellow countrymen seeking a better life in Canada.

The contradiction at play is striking. On the one hand, these well-established individuals often criticize newcomers for their perceived shortcomings, attributing these to cultural differences or a lack of understanding of Canadian norms. On the other hand, they exploit these same newcomers for financial gain, capitalizing on their vulnerabilities and aspirations.

The power dynamic in this exploitation is undeniable. Well-established individuals hold a position of authority and influence within the community. They often portray themselves as gatekeepers of knowledge and opportunity, which can be intimidating for newcomers who are still finding their footing in a new country. This power dynamic is frequently used to justify the high fees they charge for services related to immigration, even though these fees far exceed what is reasonable or fair.

By exploiting aspiring immigrants while simultaneously denouncing them, these well-established individuals perpetuate harmful stereotypes and biases. They contribute to a climate of division and mistrust within the community, which can have lasting consequences.

Getting Up Close with the Community

As I made one final attempt to get in touch with the reality in Canada, my journey led me to a remarkable encounter with a transport company that had Punjabi-origin partners as owners. These individuals were like a breath of fresh air in a world where exploitation and manipulation often tainted the hiring process for drivers. This company didn't demand money for the Labor Market Impact Assessment (LMIA) required to hire foreign workers, and this was a rarity.

Determined to unravel their story, I yearned not only to meet the owners but also to interact with their staff to understand the workings of a company that defied the norm. They graciously offered me the opportunity to travel from Toronto to Vancouver, a journey spanning approximately 4,400 km and lasting four days, in one of their massive trailer trucks. I needed special insurance, which they arranged and paid for.

My travel companion was a young man of merely 22 years, a diligent and hardworking individual who hailed from Haryana, India. Four years ago, when he first set foot in Canada, he couldn't speak Punjabi, the predominant language in many Punjabi-run companies. Still, he persevered, learning the language by immersion as he worked for a company where Punjabi was the lingua franca.

Before obtaining his truck driver's license, this young man embarked on a different journey when he first arrived in Canada.

He had initially come to Canada as a student, seeking education and a brighter future. Like many international students, he required part-time employment and lodging to support his studies and living expenses.

In the pursuit of his dream to become a truck driver, he realized that obtaining a truck driver's license in Canada was a substantial financial undertaking. The expensive training required for this endeavor meant that he had to put in extra hours at work to save up for the necessary courses and examinations. His days were a blur of academic commitments, part-time work, and the unrelenting pursuit of his goal.

His experiences with his employer were nothing short of bewildering. 'That family gave me a job when I needed it the most,' he began, 'but their mindset was stuck somewhere in the 1970s.' As he continued, I couldn't help but listen intently, curious about what he had witnessed.

'Their views about India, the Indian government, and how things function in India were completely outdated,' he explained. 'They occasionally visited their villages in India, carrying gifts for their relatives. Back home, people respected them both due to Indian cultural norms and their wealth.'

He paused for a moment, and I sensed a tinge of sadness in his voice. 'I suspect they never had their beliefs challenged because everyone back in their villages had a vested interest. They hoped these Canadian relatives would host their children when they arrived in Canada, thinking it would save them money and provide security in a new land.' With a somber expression, he continued, 'Little did they know that their children would be exploited and made to work as unpaid laborers, all in the name of providing security and shelter.'

His eyes bore the weight of this revelation, and I could see he was deeply affected by what he had witnessed in the household of his former employers. 'I thought they acted as if they had never seen money despite being wealthy,' he confessed, 'especially when it came to sharing the benefits with their young relatives who had recently arrived from India.'

His story opened my eyes to a dimension of the immigrant experience I had never considered. The struggle of newcomers, the expectations placed on them by family back home, and the exploitation they often faced in the name of protection and support were issues that demanded attention.

Our journey rolled on, and as the sun dipped below the horizon, we pulled into one of the many truck-stops that dotted the highway. In the four-day journey, we had to spend three nights like this, with the truck stops becoming our temporary haven. Inside the truck's cabin, there were bunk beds, just enough space to stretch out and rest our tired bodies. The refrigerator, stocked with delicious Indian food we had purchased in Brampton before setting out, offered a semblance of home on the road. The microwave provided comfort, as it warmed our meals and extended our time for meaningful discussions during these stops.

As we settled in for the night, I discovered a slice of the trucker's life that was unknown to me before. In Canada, truck drivers must take an eight-hour halt to rest and rejuvenate. After enduring the grueling stretches of the road, we were thoroughly drained and found ourselves with little energy for extensive conversation during our rest breaks. Our primary objectives shifted toward savoring a meal and maximizing precious moments of rest, prioritizing sleep above all else.

In the early morning hours, we'd rouse ourselves from our makeshift beds, refuel the truck, and stock up on essentials like coffee and doughnuts. The driver had a penchant for playing soothing music, and his favorite artist was Sartaj, the melodious Punjabi singer known for his profound poetry. The music lent an ambiance of serenity to the otherwise relentless journey.

As the miles rolled by and the highway stretched ahead of us, the young trucker often fell into contemplative moods. He would talk about his family, especially his parents back in India, and his sister, who was pursuing her education there. The future of his sister was a matter close to his heart, and he was determined to do everything within his power to secure her a bright one.

What struck me most about this young man was his remarkable sense of responsibility. Despite his age, he exhibited a level of maturity and dedication that was truly admirable. In his driving, he was extraordinarily careful, adhering to traffic rules and avoiding reckless behavior. It was evident that he had received comprehensive training, and he had imbibed those lessons well.

He spoke highly of the company he worked for, emphasizing that there was no divide between employees of different age groups or backgrounds. Within the company, they valued merit above all else, and he had never felt any discrimination based on his background or age. This starkly contrasted with his previous experience working for a well-heeled family as a student, where he had been subjected to a different kind of treatment.

With a tinge of melancholy, he recounted how the family he had worked for had never allowed him to share the same table as themselves. The deeply ingrained class divide, reminiscent of the kind that existed in India when that family must have first migrated to Canada, left an indelible mark on his psyche. If ever they permitted him the luxury of sitting at a table, they made sure to place him at a chair far removed from their own. Though this must have been a painful experience, he was grateful for the steady job they had offered him when he needed it the most.

I didn't press him for more details, sensing that he had shared what he felt comfortable sharing. His ability to take life's challenges in his stride and maintain a positive outlook deeply impressed me. He harbored optimism for his future and spoke of how he ensured to speak to his mother twice a day, reassuring her of his safety and well-being. It's also worth noting that he was a vegetarian, a non-smoker, and abstained from alcohol. These personal choices revealed his commitment to a healthy and disciplined lifestyle.

As I talk of this young man, I am tempted to reveal his name in admiration of his resilience and character. Yet, the fear of potential repercussions holds me back. Our journey continued, the miles stretched ahead, and the bond between us deepened, fostering a sense of camaraderie and shared experiences that transcended words.

Our journey from Toronto to Vancouver was an epic road trip that took us through diverse landscapes, showcasing the stunning tapestry of Canada's geography. We departed from Toronto, with its bustling streets and urban sprawl, and as we ventured further westward, the scenery began to transform before our very eyes.

Our route led us through the Thunder Bay district, specifically along Highway 17, also known as the Trans-Canada Highway. This stretch winds its way along the northern shores of the Great Lakes, providing a unique perspective of this massive freshwater expanse. It's a part of the Trans-Canada Highway known as the 'Lake Superior Circle Tour'. As we journeyed along this route, the landscape shifted dramatically, revealing the breathtaking transition from the forested beauty of Ontario to the vast expanse of the Canadian Prairies.

The scenery changed gradually but dramatically as we left the forested embrace of Ontario behind. Rolling hills gave way to open horizons as we entered the grand prairies. The change in topography was marked by the transition from dense forests and hilly terrain to expansive, open plains that stretched as far as the eye could see. This is where the true grandeur of the Canadian Prairies began to unfurl.

Our path took us through the province of Manitoba, which is aptly known as the 'Land of 100,000 Lakes'. We marveled at the crystal-clear waters and the abundance of lush vegetation that seemed to spring from every corner of the landscape. As we continued our westward journey, the fields became more prominent, and the air was filled with the sweet scent of earth and growing crops.

Saskatchewan, known for its sweeping fields of wheat, welcomed us with open arms. The province is often referred to as the 'Breadbasket of Canada' due to its extensive agricultural contributions, and it was a sight to behold. As we traversed this vast region, we were surrounded by the golden waves of wheat fields that seemed to stretch endlessly in all directions. The fields rippled like a sea of gold beneath the boundless blue sky.

The landscape was dotted with charming farmhouses, barns, and silos, standing as steadfast sentinels of the agricultural heritage of the province. The sun cast a warm glow on the fields, making the scene even more picturesque. Occasionally, we passed by farmers tending to their crops, their tractors rolling through the fields like modern-day chariots of agriculture.

The fields of wheat, stretching out to the horizon, whispered the story of the prairie heartland. As the wind blew gently through the vast expanse, the golden sheaths of wheat swayed in harmony, creating a symphony of rustling whispers. It was as if nature itself was reciting poetry, each rustle and sway a stanza in the tale of these boundless fields.

We couldn't help but feel a profound sense of connection to the land as we drove through this remarkable part of Saskatchewan. The landscape was more than a sight to behold; it testified the dedication and hard work of the prairie farmers who toiled tirelessly to cultivate their rich harvests. We spoke earlier about how the Ukranian-origin community helped develop this area. It was a reminder that, even in this modern age, the soul of the prairies remained rooted in the land, in the cycles of planting, growth, and harvest that have shaped this region for generations.

As we continued our journey through Saskatchewan, the vastness of the prairies seemed to stretch endlessly in all directions. It was a landscape that inspired reflection, a place where one could find solace in the expanse and tranquillity. The feeling of being a small part of this immense natural tapestry was both humbling and awe-inspiring.

The landscape told a story of resilience, of communities that thrived in harmony with the land, and of the enduring spirit of the prairies. We couldn't help but be captivated by the beauty and grandeur of the Canadian Prairies, a region where the horizon knows no bounds and the fields of wheat reach out to the sky.

We had to take a longer route as we had to pass through Calgary to change the load. As we left the vibrant city of Calgary behind, our truck embarked on a breathtaking journey through the heart of the Canadian Rockies, heading towards the Pacific jewel of Vancouver. The landscape transformed dramatically, with towering mountains that seemed to scrape the heavens. We wound our way through the formidable peaks, their snow-capped crowns glistening in the brilliant alpine sunlight. Majestic glaciers clung to the rugged terrain, their frozen rivers carving a picturesque landscape beneath. The pristine, azure lakes that adorned this rugged terrain added a touch of serenity to the awe-inspiring scenery. These clear, mirror-like bodies of water perfectly reflected the surrounding mountain giants, creating a mesmerizing and almost surreal vista.

The highway snaked through this rugged paradise, and each turn unveiled a new postcard-worthy scene. We couldn't help but pause, our senses overwhelmed by the grandeur of it all. This leg of the journey from Calgary to Vancouver was a testament to nature's unrivaled beauty, where the sheer scale of the mountains, the crystalline lakes, and the pristine glaciers served as a humbling reminder of the Earth's remarkable diversity. It was a voyage that etched indelible memories of natural wonder and left an enduring impression of the magnificence of the Canadian Rockies.

As our truck rumbled on, the vast expanse of the Canadian landscape unfurling before us, I couldn't help but reflect on the complexities of this journey. I was eager to learn more about the transport company owners and their commitment to fair labor practices and to delve deeper into the stories of those who had crossed continents in search of a better life. The road ahead was long, both literally and metaphorically, and I was ready to explore it with an open heart and a quest for understanding.

The opportunity to meet the owners of the trucking company, two brothers at the helm of this impressive operation, was an enlightening prospect. Despite the distances they had already traveled, both physically and in terms of their journey to success, there was much more to discover. The two brothers had agreed to sit down and share their remarkable story.

It was a bright and sunny day when we finally arrived at the loading bay of the transport company in Vancouver. The place was a bustling hub of activity, with trucks and trailers coming and going, a testament to the thriving business that the brothers had built from the ground up. We were welcomed into their modest office, where the scent of freshly brewed tea hung in the air.

The elder brother, Raj, leaned back in his chair and welcomed us with a warm smile. 'We're delighted to have you here,' he said. 'It's not every day that someone takes such a keen interest in our journey.'

The younger brother, Suraj, nodded in agreement. 'We've come a long way, but it's not something we talk about often. Perhaps it's time our story is heard,' he added.

Their tale of resilience and unwavering determination began in the 1990s when they made the life-altering decision to migrate from India to Canada. While the immigration process may not have been as complex as it is today, it was far from easy. Their faces bore the wisdom of the years, etched with the memories of hardships they had weathered.

Raj began, 'We started like many others, with odd jobs to make ends meet. It was challenging, to say the least. We drove taxis for a while, trying to improve our income. But we had our sights set on something bigger, something that would allow us to secure a future for ourselves and our families.'

Suraj chimed in, 'That's when we ventured into the world of trucking. It wasn't a smooth transition by any means. We faced our share of struggles and uncertainties. But we were driven by our determination to succeed and an insatiable hunger for a better life.'

Raj continued, 'After a few years of hard work and perseverance, we had an idea. Why not start our own transport company? It was a bold move, but we were ready to take that leap.'

Suraj's eyes gleamed with pride as he recounted their early days. 'The biggest hurdle we faced was raising capital. Banks were reluctant to extend credit, and we had no substantial collateral to offer. All we had in our favor was the determination to succeed and the burning desire to turn our vision into a reality.'

Raj nodded. 'We turned to relatives, friends, and other sources for loans, many of which came with heavy interest rates. We were in a tough spot, but we wouldn't back down.'

Suraj interjected, 'We're glad to report that we returned every penny, principal and interest, to those who had given us loans purely on faith and trust. In fact, to some of those who had shown trust in us, we even offered a share in the company, and we still pay them regularly.'

Their story was one of persistence, of two brothers who had transformed adversity into opportunity. They had managed to build a transport company that now boasted of hundreds of trucks and trailers. The scale of their success was awe-inspiring.

Raj leaned forward, his eyes filled with a quiet pride. 'It wasn't easy, but the journey has been worth every struggle. We've built a company that provides employment to many, and we're proud of that.' Suraj added, 'We've always believed in merit, in giving opportunities to those who work hard, just like we did. The company has employees from diverse backgrounds, not just Punjabis or white Canadians. We've always hired based on a person's abilities and dedication.'

As we delved deeper into the complexities of their operation,

I couldn't help but turn the conversation towards a topic that had been on my mind since I began my exploration – the Temporary Foreign Worker Program and the Labor Market Impact Assessments (LMIA) as well as the financial implications for immigrants. I broached the subject cautiously, aware of its sensitivity. 'I'd like to understand your perspective on LMIA and the financial aspects involved,' I began. 'It's a topic that often raises concerns, and I'm curious to know how your company views it.'

Raj, the elder brother, leaned forward and met my gaze with a serious expression. 'It's a valid concern,' he admitted. 'We've never seen our need to seek skilled workers as a means to exploit immigrants. We need the right people to run the company and scale up operations. When we apply for LMIA, we do so because we need individuals with specific skills that are essential to our operations.'

Suraj chimed in, 'It's a matter of pride for us that 80% of the people we've hired in the last 20 years are still working with us. We don't look for just anyone; we look for people with the right skills and the right attitude.'

I was intrigued by their commitment to hiring based on skills, and I probed further. 'Could you give me an example of how this works in practice? How do you decide whom to hire?'

Raj nodded and began to explain, 'Sure. Let's say we need experienced truck drivers. We consider applicants from all backgrounds, including those from South Asian countries. But it's not about their ethnicity; it's about their experience and qualifications.'

Suraj added, 'For instance, we've hired drivers from the UAE. These drivers might have South Asian origins, but they have substantial experience handling similar trucks and trailers in the UAE. They're accustomed to driving on the right side of the road, which is crucial for our operations here.'

Their approach appeared to prioritize skills and experience over anything else, and it was evident that their intention was not to exploit but to ensure a seamless integration of qualified individuals into their workforce.

I couldn't help but express my curiosity regarding the process of bringing in international talent and ensuring their legal compliance. 'Could you share more about how you assist these international hires, particularly with legal matters, and how you ensure they are accurately representing their qualifications?'

Raj leaned back, contemplating the question before answering. 'When we decide to hire someone from abroad, there's a legal process that involves verifying their credentials and ensuring they meet the required qualifications. We take that responsibility seriously. We provide legal assistance to ensure that the paperwork is in order.'

Suraj added, 'Additionally, we conduct thorough background checks to verify their qualifications and work history. We also ensure that their representations are accurate. It's a part of our commitment to ethical employment practices.'

Their meticulous approach seemed to be built on a foundation of transparency and fairness, ensuring that those they hired were not only skilled but also honest about their qualifications. I found their stance on immigrant employment practices to be refreshingly fair and ethical. It was evident that the brothers took immense pride in providing opportunities to skilled individuals, regardless of their background. Their journey, from humble beginnings to the establishment of a successful company, was not just a testament to their hard work but also to the values that guided them on their path to success. Their commitment to merit-based hiring, legal compliance, and ethical practices set an example worth emulating.

Our conversation continued to traverse the intricate landscape of immigrant employment and the challenges faced by newcomers to Canada. I was intrigued by the brothers' dedication to ethical business practices and their commitment to adhering to the laws, which begged the question of why so many other employers chose to exploit immigrants. With genuine curiosity, I asked, 'If you're doing your business ethically and following the rules, why do you think there are still so many employers who choose to exploit immigrants in this system?'

Raj, the elder brother, leaned forward, his expression serious. 'That's a complex question,' he admitted. 'The truth is there's a lot of money to be made in exploiting the system. Some employers see the potential to make a quick buck each year by "selling" employment opportunities, but we have a different outlook. We're ambitious, and we're here for the long haul. We want to sustain our business and keep growing. We steer clear of shortsighted solutions or seeking immediate gains.'

Suraj chuckled and added, 'You see, it's a matter of perspective. Maybe those employers who exploit the system are unable to generate LMIAs regularly, so they want to cash in on the few they can get their hands on. It's a short-sighted approach, driven by immediate gains.'

Raj nodded in agreement, 'There's another aspect to consider. Some employers may have experienced exploitation themselves when they first arrived in Canada. They must have been charged money and subjected to unfair practices, and now they feel it's their right to do the same. It's a cycle that perpetuates itself.'

Suraj's tone turned reflective as he continued, 'In our case, we don't want to set a bad example for our children. They have their aspirations and are not looking to join our business, but they want to work in fields like medical science or law with the primary aim of helping their communities. It's about providing legal help and guidance, not just making money. This is the legacy we want to pass on.'

Their perspective was indeed impressive. It was a viewpoint that considered the broader implications of their actions, not just the immediate benefits. Suraj added, 'It seems to me that while we can't dictate why others should or should not charge immigrants for employment opportunities, it's crucial to recognize that employees are not just in need of a job, viewed as a desperate requirement. Instead, they contribute to the growth of the business and provide their services to the company. It's a mutual relationship. Unfortunately, employers often lead immigrants to believe that it's solely their need rather than a symbiotic partnership. Sometimes, even when you tell a prospective employee that you'll obtain the required paperwork for them without charging, they might not trust you because they believe those who charge have an interest in "settling" them, whereas your focus is on providing a fair opportunity.'

Raj nodded, 'He has hit the nail on the head. It can be astonishing, but it's a fact. We often find it difficult to explain our approach. We have a respected law firm and consultant handling our cases, and they wouldn't allow us shortcuts. We must follow a procedure. Our emphasis is on growing the company.'

Suraj chimed in, 'We are no immigration consultants, and assisting immigration is not our purpose. If skilled labor is available locally, we would certainly hire it, regardless of the community it comes from. But in our field, it often isn't readily available, and we have to look beyond our borders.'

Their approach, rooted in fairness and integrity, resonated with my own belief in the potential for mutually beneficial relationships between employers and employees. I told them, 'Your story and your advice are invaluable, not just to your peers in the industry but to employers across Canada. By looking at long-term gains rather than short-term ones, you set a positive example and contribute to the growth of your company and also that of the nation.'

'We're all grateful to this country for giving us the opportunity to grow, and it's heartening to know that a new generation of hardworking individuals is looking at us for guidance if not employment,' the elder brother said.

Raj's eyes sparkled with conviction. 'We must set the right examples for the future,' he declared. 'Our legacy is more than just business success; it's about ethical practices and the impact we make on the lives of those who seek opportunities here.'

As our conversation continued, it was abundantly clear that the two brothers had not only built a thriving business but also fostered a sense of responsibility and integrity within their industry. Their journey—from immigrants who had faced their challenges to successful entrepreneurs who upheld ethical standards—was a testament to the resilience and determination of individuals who had come to Canada in search of a better life. Their story was an inspiration, not just for those within their field but for anyone seeking to make a lasting, positive impact on their community and the world.

I couldn't help but feel a profound sense of wishfulness during this enlightening conversation. It was a wish that extended far beyond the inspiring words of the two brothers, Raj and Suraj, and their commitment to ethical business practices. It was a desire that the sentiment of empathy and inclusion I had encountered in this office in Vancouver could find its way into the hearts of those I had met earlier in Brampton and Mississauga.

The haters I had encountered in those places had cast a shadow of negativity upon the younger generation of immigrants, painting them as burdens or even parasites on the system. It was a stark contrast to the reality I was witnessing now. The brothers, much like numerous individuals I encountered on my journey, were not driven by exploitative motives; instead, they were committed to diligent work, aiding immigrants in improving their own lives and their families' well-being and actively contributing to the Canadian economy.

I wished that those who held negative opinions about immigrants, especially the youth, could see beyond stereotypes and preconceived notions. If only they could witness the unwavering determination, the sense of responsibility, and the willingness to adapt and grow that I had encountered in so many individuals on this journey.

It was a hope that the broader narrative could shift – that the haters could be reached by the stories of those who, like the two brothers, had overcome their share of challenges and were now actively participating in the growth and prosperity of Canada. The wish was for a more inclusive and empathetic society, one where newcomers were recognized not as burdens but as potential contributors who had much to offer, both to their communities and to the nation.

At that moment, with the dynamic brothers, Raj and Suraj, as the embodiment of progress and determination, I felt compelled to delve into a question that had perplexed me throughout my journey: why did some earlier immigrants harbor negative sentiments towards newcomers and how could we bridge the gap to foster better relations between them? It was a question that weighed heavily on my mind, and I knew that these two individuals, with their wisdom and perspective, were the right ones to answer it.

With a sense of curiosity, I posed the question: 'Why do you think there's a divide between earlier immigrants and newcomers, and how can we work to improve these relationships?'

Raj, ever thoughtful, leaned forward as if to absorb the depth of the question. 'We've never really realized that such a divide exists,' he admitted. 'We've been occupied with improving our own lives and those of our employees. We've never viewed the new immigrants as a threat or a nuisance. Perhaps that's the fundamental difference.'

Suraj nodded in agreement, reflecting on the matter.

'It's possible that those harboring negative feelings are individuals who have little to occupy their lives. By denouncing this newer generation, they may derive a misplaced sense of accomplishment. It's a veil to conceal their lack of achievements, a way to feel superior. Those who've attained remarkable success understand the price that comes with it and, more often than not, appreciate the ambition and effort of those who come to Canada with the intent of changing their lives.' Their perspective was enlightening, revealing that these two brothers, despite their substantial success, felt they had achieved just a fraction of what they had aspired to. Their ongoing efforts spoke to a continuous quest for self-improvement.

Raj shared further insights, acknowledging the diversity among immigrants. 'We understand that within every group of a few hundred people who come to Canada, there may be individuals who are not particularly suitable for employment. However, by and large, immigrants are often driven and self-motivated. They've left the comfort of their homes, embraced risks to seek a better life, and they mitigate these risks through hard work.'

Suraj suggested, 'Perhaps the detractors shouldn't be taken too seriously. It's easy for us to say, but their disdainful behavior, as if they belong to a superior race than the current immigrants, can be quite hurtful.'

I couldn't help but convey my concerns about this matter, emphasizing how these individuals, whom I had come to refer to as the 'brown-goras', often demonstrated discriminatory attitudes, believing that they had become the white Canadians whom they served when they first came to this land a few decades ago. They had racist attitudes towards their community. I informed them how the younger community doesn't get the same animosity from the other Canadians, irrespective of their origins. I even pointed out instances in the Indian language media and even shared some YouTube videos as evidence.

The brothers sighed, acknowledging the validity of my concerns. 'We see your point,' Raj admitted. 'While these people may have made significant progress in their own lives and that of their families, collectively contributing to the Canadian economy, they might not be high achievers as individuals. This, we believe, is where the crucial difference lies. High achievers tend to seek further accomplishments rather than sit back and criticize others.'

The conversation with Raj and Suraj, as insightful as it was, evoked a memory from a previous chapter where I had delved into the concept of Social Identity Theory—how individuals tend to boost their self-esteem through the process of out-group discrimination, a phenomenon closely connected to our perception of self-worth relative to others. The similarity between the theory and the brothers' perspective was striking.

One of the central ideas in the theory is that people tend to categorize themselves into social groups based on shared characteristics, be it nationality, ethnicity, religion, or any other distinguishing factor. The theory posits that individuals often identify with their in-group and the group they belong to and derive a sense of self-esteem from this association. In contrast, they view out-groups, those they don't belong to, as the 'other' and sometimes discriminate against them to elevate their self-worth.

Raj and Suraj, in their candid responses, had echoed a similar sentiment. They never saw newer immigrants as the 'other' or a threat to their sense of achievement and identity. Instead, they had a deep appreciation for the ambition and hard work of those who came to Canada seeking a better life. They understood the challenges and sacrifices made by immigrants because they themselves had been through it. This sense of empathy and shared experience made them less likely to indulge in out-group discrimination, as suggested by the Social Identity Theory.

The theory also highlights that when individuals feel a need to boost their self-esteem, they may resort to out-group derogation, which involves belittling or discriminating against members of out-groups to feel better about themselves. However, Raj and Suraj seemed to have taken a different path. They did not feel the need to put down newer immigrants to elevate their self-esteem. Instead, they recognized the value and potential of the newcomers and appreciated their contributions to Canadian society. This contrasted starkly with the behaviors of those I had encountered earlier, who exhibited a need to establish themselves as 'better' or more integrated into the host culture by discriminating against their fellow immigrants.

Raj and Suraj had, in their own words and through their actions, provided a real-world example that added depth and richness to the theoretical framework of the Social Identity Theory. Their perspective sheds light on the dynamics of in-group and out-group categorization, self-esteem enhancement, and the real-life implications of these concepts.

As our conversation continued, they astutely pointed out that the individuals I had encountered earlier, whom I had referred to as 'haters', were essentially treating the newer immigrants as the out-group. In doing so, they were engaging in behaviors such as denouncing, belittling, and criticizing these newcomers. It was a means for these individuals to bolster their self-esteem by creating a perceived divide and establishing themselves as part of a superior in-group. Raj and Suraj's candid observations and lived experiences breathed life into the abstract concepts of Social Identity Theory. They were, in essence, living examples of how the dynamics of in-group and out-group categorization played out in the real world. The 'haters' were using out-group discrimination as a means to boost their self-esteem, while the two brothers chose a different path.

By recognizing the shared experiences and aspirations of the newcomers, Raj and Suraj demonstrated that there was no need to resort to out-group derogation to elevate one's self-worth. Their approach was rooted in empathy, collaboration, and a belief in the collective advancement of their community. They dispelled the need for divisive behavior and highlighted the power of unity and mutual support within the immigrant population.

Bridging Divides: Uniting Indian Immigrant Generations

In the heart of vibrant communities across Canada, from Vancouver to Brampton, places of worship serve as much more than just that. Particularly for Indian immigrants, both new and established, they are beacons of support and solidarity, centers of community life, pulsating with a shared spirit, always providing a helping hand to newcomers and students, and offering vital material assistance.

Presently, they stand ready to expand their horizons and extend new services, such as career counseling and legal guidance, thereby equipping the Indian immigrant community to flourish and contribute to Canadian society. Those members of the community who have found success and fulfillment in their adopted homeland can channel their efforts toward the many goals outlined in the succeeding paragraphs. By embracing the concepts of unity, shared values, and cultural diversity, the Indian immigrant community in Canada is poised to not only enrich its collective experience but to leave a profound and lasting imprint on the broader Canadian mosaic. This chapter offers practical insights, guidance, and a roadmap for the journey ahead as we strive to build a stronger, more harmonious, and closely-knit Indian community.

In the late 1970s through the early 2000s, waves of Indian immigrants embarked on a journey to Canada, seeking better opportunities, a brighter future, and a chance to create a new home far from the shores of their native land. For these pioneers, the transition to a foreign land was marked by countless trials and tribulations, but it was a path paved with dreams of prosperity and the promise of a better life. They were the torchbearers of a legacy that would continue for generations to come, forming the foundation of an Indian diaspora in Canada. Little did they know that their descendants, the new generation of Indian immigrants, would enter a world so different and yet so interconnected, a world where the echoes of their heritage would resonate alongside the rhythms of modernity.

As part of my journey in writing this book, I delved into the complex, often contentious, relationship between the earlier Indian immigrants and the ones currently arriving in Canada. A deep curiosity drove me to understand the dynamics of this generational divide. What I discovered was a story of nostalgia, insecurity, and, in some instances, a sense of disillusionment.

The sentiments expressed by the earlier Indian immigrants toward the present generation can only be described as complex and, at times, marred by a disdain that transcends mere disagreement. During my research, I engaged in candid conversations with both groups, listening to their perspectives and experiences. What emerged was a poignant narrative of how the past and the present coexist in a delicate dance of cultural identities, expectations, and misunderstandings.

The disdain and sometimes resentment harbored by the earlier Indian immigrants toward the newcomers is rooted in a series of misperceptions and generalizations. These pioneers often held negative feelings towards the new generation, a sentiment that, regrettably, was reciprocated. They accused the newer immigrants of numerous transgressions, including driving the crime rate higher. However, when probed for concrete evidence or statistical support for this claim, a void emerged. In many ways, this accusation was not substantiated by empirical data or objective analysis but fuelled by a fear of the unknown, a common human tendency to be apprehensive about change, especially when it involves something as intimate as one's cultural heritage.

The disdain often manifested in seemingly minor complaints, such as the cleanliness of toilets at concerts featuring Punjabi singers. The truth is that issues related to restroom cleanliness at concerts, especially ones attended by enthusiastic teenagers and young adults, can be attributed more to a skewed attendee-to-toilet ratio and the general behavior typical of such events rather than the nationality of the performers or the attendees. However, this otherwise ordinary concern seemed to be blown out of proportion when it was directed at the newcomers. The older generation, many of whom had never attended a concert outside of their own community, resorted to blaming their own people rather than recognizing the universal nature of such issues.

The peculiar aspect of this generational divide was that it wasn't a blanket indictment of the next generation but focused on the next generation of immigrants from India, a distinction that underscores the complexity of the issue.

So, why is it so important to bridge this gap between the earlier Indian immigrants and the new arrivals? The significance of fostering unity and cohesion within the Indian immigrant community lies in that these generational divides lead to isolation, mistrust, and the loss of a valuable support network that the community could otherwise provide. It's vital to understand that these divides not only affect the relationship between the generations but also have broader implications for the Indian diaspora. By overcoming them, we create a stronger, more united community that can effectively advocate for its members, share cultural richness, and contribute positively to society, whether in Canada or anywhere else.

One way to address the generational divide within the Indian immigrant community in Canada is to delve into the historical context of Indian immigration worldwide and examine the evolution of the Indian diaspora everywhere.

Historical Context of Indian Immigration and the Evolution of the Indian Diaspora Worldwide

Both struggle and success mark the history of Indian immigration, and it stretches back to the nineteenth century. The first significant wave of Indian immigrants ventured beyond their homeland to various parts of the world, driven by a complex interplay of economic, social, and political factors. Their journey was often fraught with hardship, yet it laid the groundwork for the vast diaspora across the world that we see today. While Canada is home to one segment of this diaspora, the story of Indian immigration unfolds across multiple continents.

In the United States, for instance, Indian immigration traces back to the early twentieth century. Like their Canadian counterparts, Indian immigrants in the US initially faced considerable prejudice and discrimination. However, over the years, they have carved out a prominent place in various fields, including technology, medicine, and business. Today, Indian Americans are recognized for their significant contributions to American society.

In the United Kingdom, Indian immigration has deep roots, dating back to the colonial era. Indian immigrants in the UK have played a pivotal role in shaping British culture, particularly in the realm of cuisine, and have been influential in various sectors, including politics and the arts.

In the Persian Gulf countries, Indian expatriates have flocked to the region for economic opportunities, primarily in the fields of construction, healthcare, and hospitality. These expatriates often send remittances back to India, providing a vital source of income for their families.

These are a few examples of the global Indian diaspora's evolution. The experiences, challenges, and contributions of immigrants have been as diverse as the countries they have settled in, reflecting the broader narrative of Indian migration worldwide.

Factors Contributing to the Divide

The generational divide within the Indian immigrant community in Canada is not a unique phenomenon; it reflects patterns seen in diaspora communities across the world. To truly bridge this divide, it is crucial to recognize the factors that contribute to it, which encompass cultural, social, and economic aspects.

Cultural Factors

Cultural identity plays a significant role in the division between the earlier and newer generations of Indian immigrants. The earlier immigrants often came to Canada with a strong attachment to their homeland and its traditions. They have preserved their cultural heritage diligently, fostering a sense of nostalgia for the 'homeland' that sometimes makes it challenging to adapt to the changes that the modern world and the new generation bring.

Conversely, the new generation of Indian immigrants may have a more fluid sense of cultural identity influenced by the multicultural milieu of Canada. They may embrace a more diverse and evolving understanding of their Indian heritage, which can be perceived as a threat to the traditions held dear by their parents and grandparents.

Social Factors

Social dynamics, including the communities in which these immigrants reside, have a profound impact on their generational differences. The earlier immigrants built close-knit communities bound together by shared traditions and languages. This isolation, while providing comfort and familiarity, can sometimes lead to a lack of exposure to the broader Canadian society.

The new generation, on the other hand, is often more integrated into mainstream Canadian society, as they attend local schools, interact with peers from different backgrounds, and engage in various aspects of Canadian life. This integration can sometimes be seen as a dilution of the cultural identity held by the earlier generation, leading to feelings of discomfort and occasional apprehension.

Economic Factors

Economic disparities, both within the Indian community and compared to the broader Canadian society, also contribute to this generational divide. The earlier immigrants, who often came with limited resources, faced significant challenges in establishing themselves in a new country. They worked tirelessly to build a better future for their families and, in many cases, succeeded.

The new generation of Indian immigrants is entering Canada in a different economic landscape. They often benefit from the educational and professional opportunities that their parents and grandparents worked hard to secure. This economic advantage can sometimes create resentment among the earlier generation, some of whom perceive it as ungratefulness for their sacrifices and hard work.

Understanding these cultural, social, and economic factors that contribute to the generational divide is the first step towards bridging this gap. By acknowledging the complexities of the Indian immigrant experience in Canada, we can begin to chart a course for fostering unity, shared understanding, and mutual respect within the community.

The Out-group Mentality – Navigating In-group and Out-group Dynamics

While we delved into this topic previously, I briefly touch upon it here again because a comprehensive grasp of the generational gap within the Canadian Indian immigrant community necessitates an exploration of the 'in-group' and 'out-group' dynamics, especially in the context of the Indian diaspora. These sociological terms offer valuable insights into why earlier immigrants may perceive recent arrivals as outsiders and the broader implications of such a mentality on both individuals and communities.

Exploring the Concept of In-group and Out-group

In the realm of sociology and social psychology, the concepts of 'in-group' and 'out-group' are pivotal in comprehending how individuals perceive and interact with those around them. An 'in-group' refers to a social group with which an individual identifies and feels a sense of belonging. Typically, it includes people who share common characteristics, experiences, or affiliations. In contrast, an out-group consists of individuals who are perceived as different from the in-group, often based on various criteria, such as race, ethnicity, nationality, or generation.

Within the Indian immigrant community in Canada, these concepts are highly relevant. The earlier immigrants, who laid the foundations of the community from the 1970s to the early 2000s, naturally established their own in-group. Shared experiences of migration, cultural traditions, and a profound sense of camaraderie characterized this group. They built a community bound together by the challenges they collectively overcame and the milestones they celebrated as one.

On the other hand, the newer generation of Indian immigrants, owing to their later arrival and broader range of experiences and influences, can be perceived as part of a different in-group. In some cases, this generational divide leads to the perception that the newer arrivals belong to an out-group, implying that they are 'foreign' or 'different.'

The inclination of earlier Indian immigrants to view their more recent counterparts as outsiders is rooted in several factors, and the educational advancements of the new generation are a key contributing factor.

Fear of Change and the Unknown

Human beings often fear what they do not understand or what is different from what they are accustomed to. The earlier immigrants might view the cultural attitudes, values, and behaviors of the new generation as foreign and unfamiliar. This fear can lead to a sense of estrangement, as the known and familiar ways of their generation differ from the ways of their descendants.

Nostalgia and Cultural Preservation

Nostalgia for one's cultural roots is a potent force. The earlier generation of Indian immigrants often holds their cultural identity close to their hearts. They may perceive the new generation as less connected to these traditions and, in some cases, may even view their adaptations or modifications as a threat to the preservation of their heritage.

Economic and Social Disparities

Economic disparities within the Indian immigrant community contribute to the in-group and out-group mentality. The earlier immigrants faced more significant economic challenges, and, as a result, they developed a collective identity around their struggles. When they see the new generation benefiting from educational and professional opportunities, it can create resentment and a perception that they are no longer part of the same in-group.

Communication Gaps

Communication gaps often exacerbate the divide between generations. The use of different languages or dialects, especially in multilingual households, can create barriers to understanding. The older generation may feel left out or misunderstood, further fuelling the perception that they are on the outside looking in.

Generational Gap in Values and Priorities

The evolving social and cultural values of the new generation can be a source of tension. While the earlier immigrants may hold traditional values dear, the newer generation might embrace more modern or Westernized values. This difference in values can be perceived as a distancing from the shared values of the in-group.

Educational Advancements

One notable distinction between the earlier and newer generations is the level of education. The newer generation of Indian immigrants is often better educated than their predecessors, particularly those who arrived in the 1970s and 1980s. This educational advantage is a significant contributing factor to their ability to cross borders as they navigate the stringent language proficiency tests that have become prerequisites for immigration in recent years.

Improved Conditions in India

Another significant contributing factor to the changing dynamics within the Indian immigrant community in Canada is the remarkable transformation that India itself has undergone. This transformation encompasses various aspects, including significant economic growth and profound shifts in social norms.

Perhaps one of the most striking changes lies in India's economic landscape. The per capita GDP (Gross Domestic Product per capita) of India has seen a remarkable rise over the years. In the 1970s, it hovered at a modest range, typically between $150 to $250. This low figure represented the economic challenges and limited opportunities that the earlier Indian immigrants faced in their homeland, compelling them to seek a better life abroad. In stark contrast, today, India's per capita GDP stands at around $2,250, reflecting significant economic growth and an expanded middle class.

This increase in per capita GDP is not merely a statistic; it represents improved economic prospects, educational opportunities, and living standards for the Indian population. The younger generation of Indian immigrants, who hail from this transformed India, is entering Canada with a different set of experiences. They come equipped with higher levels of education and often have a better command of the English and French languages, which are vital for successful immigration, given the stricter language proficiency requirements in recent years.

Moreover, the educational landscape in India has evolved dramatically, offering better schools, colleges, and vocational training opportunities that equip individuals with the skills necessary to compete on the global stage. This educational advantage empowers the newer generation of immigrants, allowing them to pursue diverse career paths and contribute more substantially to Canadian society.

In addition to economic growth and educational advancements, India has witnessed significant social changes. There has been a noticeable shift in social permissibility norms, allowing for greater individual freedom and fostering a broader perspective. This change has contributed to the newer generation's outlook, which often embraces diversity and values individual rights and choices.

As a result of these remarkable transformations in India, the generational gap within the Indian immigrant community becomes even more nuanced. The newer generation, benefiting from the improved conditions and opportunities in their home country, approaches life in Canada with different experiences and aspirations. Understanding these shifts and their implications is pivotal in bridging the divide and fostering unity within the Indian immigrant community.

The Impact of the Out-group Mentality on Individuals and Communities

The out-group mentality within the Indian immigrant community has wide-ranging consequences, affecting both individuals and the community. For individuals, feeling part of an out-group within their community can lead to emotional strain. It can cause anxiety, loneliness, and a sense of isolation, as individuals may feel rejected or excluded.

The new generation might struggle with a cultural identity crisis. They may feel torn between their Indian heritage and the pressures to assimilate into Canadian society. This inner conflict can affect their self-esteem and well-being.

Communication breakdowns between generations hinder the transfer of cultural knowledge and values. The out-group mentality can exacerbate these communication barriers, leading to misunderstandings and a loss of intergenerational connections. Within communities, the out-group mentality can lead to divisiveness, and when different segments of the community view each other as outsiders, it weakens the sense of unity and common purpose. When generations do not collaborate and share experiences, opportunities for learning and growth are lost. The older generation can provide valuable insights and wisdom, while the newer generation can bring fresh perspectives and innovation.

A fragmented community is less effective in advocating for its members' rights and interests. A united front is more likely to create positive change and address common concerns. The Indian immigrant community's strength lies in its cultural richness. When generations do not work together to celebrate and preserve this richness, it diminishes the community's capacity to share its heritage with the broader Canadian society.

Bridging the generational divide within the Indian immigrant community is not just about harmonizing relationships between the old and the new; it's about fostering a sense of unity and inclusion that benefits everyone. The implications of the out-group mentality are clear: it weakens the community's cohesion and potential. As we move forward, we will explore strategies for overcoming this mentality and building a more united, resilient, and culturally vibrant Indian immigrant community in Canada, where both the echoes of the past and the aspirations of the present are celebrated and embraced.

The generational divide within the Indian immigrant community in Canada has its roots in different experiences, perspectives, and expectations. However, beneath these apparent differences lies a wealth of common ground and shared values that can be harnessed to bridge this divide and create a stronger, more united community.

Identifying Common Cultural Values and Traditions

While the Indian immigrant community spans multiple generations, it remains intrinsically connected by a rich tapestry of shared cultural values and traditions. These values form the heart and soul of the community, and they serve as a common thread that binds generations together.

Family-Centred Values

Family is at the core of Indian culture. The respect for elders, the importance of close-knit families, and the sense of responsibility toward one's kin are values that both the earlier and newer generations uphold. These values transcend time and generation, offering a strong common foundation.

Celebrating Cultural Heritage

The preservation and celebration of cultural heritage are paramount to both generations. Whether it's through festivals, traditional rituals, or the passing down of cultural stories, the Indian immigrant community continues to cherish and honor its roots.

Hard Work and Resilience

The older generation is often admired for its resilience and unyielding work ethic. The values of hard work, determination, and perseverance have been passed down through the generations. The newer generation, too, carries these values forward in their pursuit of success.

Education and Learning

A commitment to education and a reverence for knowledge are values that transcend generations. Both generations recognize the transformative power of education and actively promote learning within their families.

Community and Social Responsibility

The sense of community extends beyond just familial ties. Both generations place a strong emphasis on social responsibility, often engaging in community activities, charity work, and promoting cultural exchange.

Recognizing and celebrating these common cultural values and traditions is a pivotal step in bridging the generational divide. It fosters a sense of unity and belonging, reminding individuals of their shared heritage and shared values. It also sets the stage for constructive dialogue, as both generations can draw from these common values to find solutions that work for the entire community. Each generation brings its unique strengths and contributions to the table. Acknowledging and valuing these strengths can help build respect and mutual appreciation.

Strengths of the Earlier Generation

Pioneering Spirit

The earlier immigrants demonstrated immense courage and resilience when they left their homeland to settle in a foreign country. They navigated a landscape often marked by racial discrimination and language barriers, yet they persevered and laid the foundations for future generations.

Cultural Preservation

The older generation played a vital role in preserving and passing down cultural traditions. Their commitment to it ensures that the Indian identity remains strong within the community.

Work Ethic

The earlier immigrants are renowned for their unwavering work ethic. They often took on labor-intensive jobs and built the foundation for economic success, which the newer generation now benefits from.

Resilience

The older generation faced countless challenges, and their resilience in overcoming them serves as an inspiration for the community. Their ability to adapt to a new environment and make the best of it is commendable.

Strengths of the Newer Generation

Education and Professionalism

The newer generation often comes to Canada with higher levels of education and professional qualifications. Their educational backgrounds and skills contribute significantly to the Canadian workforce and economy.

Cultural Adaptability

The newer immigrants are adept at navigating multicultural settings and are often quick to adapt to the Canadian way of life. This adaptability fosters stronger connections with the broader Canadian society.

Technological Literacy

The newer generation is typically more tech-savvy, and this expertise is valuable in a world increasingly reliant on technology.

Global Perspective

Growing up in a globalized world, the newer generation often brings a broader perspective and is more open to diverse ideas and experiences.

By highlighting the strengths and contributions of both generations, we can move away from divisive comparisons and instead focus on the complementary nature of their experiences. A collaborative approach, recognizing that each generation has unique assets, can lead to a stronger, more resilient community.

Demonstrating Shared Overarching Goals

While the paths taken by each generation may differ, their ultimate goals are remarkably similar. The pursuit of success, prosperity, and well-being is a universal aspiration that unites both the earlier and newer immigrants.

Economic Success

Both generations share the goal of achieving economic stability and success. The earlier generation paved the way for this pursuit, and the newer generation follows in their footsteps, working towards a better financial future for themselves and their families.

Education and Personal Growth

Education is a common thread connecting both generations. Whether it's the earlier generation's emphasis on knowledge or the newer generation's pursuit of academic and professional excellence, the commitment to personal growth remains constant.

Cultural Preservation

The preservation of cultural heritage is a shared goal. While the older generation seeks to safeguard and pass on traditions, the newer generation values its cultural roots and wishes to maintain its connection with India.

Quality of Life

The pursuit of a higher quality of life and overall well-being is a fundamental goal for both generations. This includes access to healthcare, a comfortable living environment, and the opportunity to enjoy the fruits of their labor.

Contribution to Society

A sense of social responsibility and the desire to make meaningful contributions to the community and the broader Canadian society are shared aspirations. Both generations recognize the importance of giving back and making a positive impact.

Demonstrating that both groups are working toward these common overarching goals underscores the interconnectedness of their experiences. This recognition can catalyze mutual understanding, empathy, and collaboration within the Indian immigrant community.

Communication and Dialogue

Effective communication lies at the heart of bridging the generational divide within the Indian immigrant community in Canada. It serves as a potent tool for promoting understanding, empathy, and cooperation between the earlier and newer generations. Communication is the linchpin that holds communities together, ensuring that individuals can connect, share, and collaborate. Within the Indian immigrant community in Canada, open and honest communication plays a vital role in fostering unity and harmony.

Breaking Down Stereotypes

Open communication enables individuals from different generations to share their perspectives, experiences, and viewpoints. This, in turn, helps to break down stereotypes and dispel misconceptions that may fuel division.

Fostering Empathy

Through dialogue, members of both generations can develop a deeper understanding of each other's hopes, dreams, and challenges. This fosters empathy, promoting the ability to see things from the other's perspective.

Building Trust

Trust is the cornerstone of any thriving community. By engaging in open, transparent conversations, both generations can build trust, knowing that they can rely on one another and work towards common goals.

Collaborative Problem-Solving

Effective communication empowers both generations to come together to solve common problems and address shared concerns. It allows them to leverage their combined knowledge, skills, and resources for the greater good.

Strategies for Facilitating Dialogue and Understanding

Certain strategies can be implemented to foster intergenerational dialogue and understanding within the Indian immigrant community. These strategies serve as bridges connecting the two generations, allowing them to cross the chasm of misunderstandings and differences, and can be implemented at various levels, for example, the City Council or at the neighborhood level or even as library activities and indeed by the media, both radio/television as well as the YouTube channels.

Community Forums

Regular community forums or gatherings can be organized, serving as platforms for open dialogue. These events should encourage individuals from both generations to express their thoughts and concerns freely.

Intergenerational Workshops

Educational workshops can be conducted to explore generational differences and similarities. These workshops can provide a safe space for open discussions and promote mutual learning.

Mentoring Programs

Mentorship programs can pair individuals from different generations, fostering mentor-mentee relationships. These partnerships enable the sharing of knowledge, experiences, and skills, contributing to a deeper understanding of each other.

Storytelling and Oral Histories

Individuals from the earlier generation ought to share their life stories, experiences, and wisdom with the newer generation. Storytelling can be a powerful tool for conveying traditions, values, and personal insights.

Collaboration on Community Projects

Both generations can actively engage in community initiatives, such as cultural events, charitable activities, and volunteer work. This shared participation promotes cooperation and a sense of shared purpose.

To illustrate the power of effective intergenerational communication, we can turn to both real-life examples and imagined scenarios. While the real-life examples showcase instances where intergenerational communication has bridged gaps in other communities, the imagined scenarios demonstrate how similar communication strategies could work within the Indian immigrant community in Canada.

Imagine a multicultural neighborhood where an annual cultural festival takes place. In the past, there have been issues between the younger and older generations within a particular ethnic group. The younger generation feels that the traditions and practices are outdated and misrepresented, while the older generation believes that the festival should adhere to the traditions of their homeland.

In response, a community council initiates a series of open forums in the months leading up to the festival. These forums bring together representatives from both generations to express their viewpoints, discuss traditions, and work together to find a balanced approach. Through these dialogues, the community manages to design a festival that respects the heritage of the older generation while embracing the contributions of the younger generation. The event became a resounding success, with both generations taking pride in their collaboration.

Now, consider an Indian immigrant community in Canada where the older generation has concerns about the cultural dilution they perceive in the younger generation. They feel that their heritage is fading as their children and grandchildren embrace Western values.

In this scenario, a forward-thinking *gurdwara*[5] takes the initiative to address these concerns. They dedicate one congregation per month to organizing dialogues between the generations. During these sessions, both generations are encouraged to discuss their aspirations and values openly. In addition, the congregation organizes activities that compel the older and newer generations to interact and understand each other better. For example, they create events where the younger generation participates in traditional cooking lessons or learns about classical Indian music while the older generation engages in discussions about contemporary social issues.

Over time, these dialogues and interactions foster a deeper understanding and appreciation for each other's perspectives. The younger generation learns to respect their cultural roots, while the older generation acknowledges the benefits of embracing change and adaptation. As a result, the gurdwara community becomes a model of intergenerational harmony, with both generations actively participating in religious and cultural activities. The same can be adopted by the Hindu temples and other religious institutes of the community since the diaspora is deeply religious.

Furthermore, it is worth noting that such activities can be extended to public spaces, including parks, in immigrant-dominated areas like Brampton. By expanding these dialogue-promoting endeavors to communal settings, they can be instrumental in fostering intergenerational understanding and harmony in broader community contexts.

---

[5] A Sikh place of worship

Celebrating Diversity

Diversity is not merely a fact of life; it's the heartbeat of any vibrant, dynamic community. Within the Indian immigrant community in Canada, the UK, Australia, and the USA, the spectrum of diversity is exceptionally wide, encompassing a myriad of regional backgrounds, languages, and cultural traditions. Embracing and celebrating this diversity fortifies the community, and the various cultural festivals and traditions serve as common ground, uniting generations in their shared heritage.

The Indian immigrant community is a kaleidoscope of experiences stemming from the diverse roots of its members. The community includes individuals and families who have arrived from various regions across India, bringing with them distinct cultural practices, languages, and traditions. While this diversity can sometimes lead to differences, it also holds the potential to be a source of strength and unity.

Cultural Plurality

The community boasts a rich tapestry of cultural traditions, including diverse cuisines, music, dance, and clothing. Each region of India has its unique contributions, reflecting the country's remarkable cultural wealth.

Language Diversity

The Indian immigrant community converses in numerous languages, with Hindi, Punjabi, Tamil, Gujarati, and Bengali, among others, being commonly spoken. This linguistic diversity is an integral part of the community's identity.

Religious Harmony

The community encompasses various religious beliefs, including Hinduism, Sikhism, Islam, Christianity, Jainism, Buddhism, and more. The coexistence of different religious faiths within the community exemplifies religious harmony.

Regional Pride

Members of the community often take great pride in their regional identities, celebrating festivals and practices unique to their home states. This regional diversity is an essential part of the community's vibrant mosaic. Celebrating it is more than just an appreciation of differences; it's about recognizing the potential that these differences hold for fostering unity and strength.

Enriched Cultural Experience

Embracing diversity offers members of the community a chance to experience a wide array of cultural traditions. From Diwali celebrations to Vaisakhi parades, different cultural festivals provide unique opportunities for learning and enrichment.

Learning and Growth

Exposure to various languages, customs, and rituals broadens horizons and encourages learning. It fosters an environment where individuals can acquire new skills and knowledge, enriching their personal growth.

Interconnectedness

Celebrating diversity can lead to deeper connections among community members. By appreciating and engaging with each other's cultural practices, individuals can forge stronger bonds and a sense of belonging.

Resilience and Adaptability

A diverse community is often more resilient and adaptable as it draws upon the strengths of its various components to overcome challenges and seize opportunities.

Showcasing Various Cultural Festivals and Traditions

Cultural festivals and traditions serve as the heartbeats of the Indian immigrant community in Canada. These events are occasions when generations come together to celebrate shared heritage, exchange experiences, and promote unity.

Diwali, the Festival of Lights, is one of the most widely celebrated festivals within the Indian community. It transcends religious and regional boundaries, uniting the community in a spirit of joy and togetherness. The festival signifies the victory of light over darkness and good over evil, making it a powerful symbol of unity. Then there is Holi, the Festival of Colours, which transcends generational divides. For the Punjabis, Vaisakhi is a significant festival celebrated with great enthusiasm. It not only commemorates the formation of the Khalsa but also highlights the importance of community service and unity. The event includes processions, martial arts demonstrations, and the sharing of communal meals. Pongal/Makar Sankranti, Eid, and Christmas and their celebrations exemplify unity and togetherness among diverse segments of the community. On Canada Day, the community joins the larger Canadian society in celebrating the nation's history and diversity. It is an occasion when generations can come together to express their shared love and appreciation for their adopted homeland.

These cultural festivals and traditions are not just annual events; they are the lifeblood of the Indian immigrant community, representing a tapestry of customs, colors, and stories. They provide opportunities for both the older and newer generations to bond over shared experiences, honor traditions, and forge lasting connections.

Let's take a practical approach to leveraging this cultural diversity to promote unity and inclusivity and further strengthen the Indian immigrant community in Canada as a vibrant, harmonious, and integrated collective.

Breaking Stereotypes

In a community as diverse as the Indian immigrant community in Canada, stereotypes and misconceptions sometimes sow seeds of division and misunderstanding. It's essential to address these stereotypes to promote empathy, dispel negative preconceptions, and ultimately build a more united and harmonious community. It is important to address stereotypes, value empathy, and the ways in which we can dispel misconceptions to lead to a stronger and more closely-knit community.

Stereotypes are oversimplified beliefs or generalizations about a particular group. Unfortunately, both the earlier and newer generations in the Indian immigrant community can, at times, hold stereotypes and misconceptions about each other.

Stereotypes of the Earlier Generation

The newer generation may sometimes stereotype the older generation as being conservative, less adaptable to change, and resistant to new ideas. They might perceive them as being more traditional and less open to embracing Western culture.

Stereotypes of the Newer Generation

On the other hand, the older generation may have misconceptions about the newer generation, viewing them as disconnected from their cultural roots, overly assimilated into Western society, and lacking respect for their heritage.

Addressing these stereotypes is essential to prevent them from deepening the generational divide, and both generations have much to offer.

Promoting Empathy and Dispelling Negative Preconceptions

Empathy is the ability to understand and share the feelings of others. In the context of the Indian immigrant community in Canada, fostering empathy between the generations is vital for dispelling stereotypes and misconceptions.

Open Dialogue

Encourage open and respectful dialogue between the generations.

Listening to each other's experiences and perspectives is a potent way to build empathy.

Walk in Each Other's Shoes

Organize events or activities that allow members of both generations to experience each other's lives. For example, the older generation can participate in activities popular with the younger generation and vice versa. This fosters mutual understanding.

Learn from Personal Stories

Personal stories and experiences can be a powerful tool for promoting empathy. Share stories that highlight the challenges, triumphs, and emotions experienced by individuals in both generations.

Seek Common Ground

Find common interests and shared values to build upon. Both generations can identify areas where they agree and collaborate to achieve common goals. Dispelling stereotypes and misconceptions is not just about creating harmony within the Indian immigrant community; it's about building a stronger and more unified community.

Unity and Collaboration

By addressing stereotypes and fostering empathy, both generations can come together, capitalizing on their strengths and shared values. This unity enables them to work together effectively to address common concerns.

Mutual Respect

Breaking stereotypes promotes mutual respect. Members of both generations recognize and value each other's contributions and perspectives.

Preservation of Culture

When stereotypes are dispelled, it becomes clear that cultural traditions can be passed on and celebrated by both generations.

The older generation can share their cultural wisdom, and the newer generation can bring fresh perspectives and innovations.

Stronger Advocacy

A united community is more effective in advocating for its rights and interests. Both generations can come together to address issues and create positive change within the community and in the broader Canadian society.

Building a United Front in the Indian Immigrant Community

In any vibrant and diverse community, unity is not just a desirable trait, it's essential for progress and prosperity, and the Indian immigrant community in Canada is no exception. Collaborative efforts bridge generational divides and create support networks that encompass both the earlier and newer generations. Together, we can harness the strength that unity offers to build a resilient, harmonious, and successful Indian immigrant community.

The Importance of Working Together

Unity is more than just a buzzword, it's the foundation upon which a thriving community is built. Working together as a united front has profound implications for the Indian immigrant community in Canada.

Amplifying Strength

Unity allows the community to draw upon the combined strengths and resources of both generations. When they work together, they become a powerful force that can address challenges and seize opportunities effectively.

Resilience

A united community is more resilient when faced with adversity. Challenges that may seem insurmountable for one generation can be overcome when both generations combine their knowledge and experiences.

Diversity in Action

The Indian immigrant community's diversity, with its multitude of languages, traditions, and skills, becomes a valuable resource when both generations collaborate. This diversity is an asset that can be harnessed for community growth and development.

Advocacy

When the community speaks with one voice, it's more effective in advocating for its rights and interests, whether it's within Canada or on issues concerning India.

Collaborative Efforts for the Greater Good

The earlier and newer generations within the Indian immigrant community each bring unique perspectives and experiences to the table. Collaborative efforts that bridge generational divides can be powerful drivers of community growth and prosperity.

Educational Initiatives

Collaborative efforts can take the form of mentorship programs where older individuals share their knowledge and experiences with younger members. This not only promotes personal growth but also strengthens the community's intellectual capital.

Cultural Exchanges

The collaborative efforts of both generations can enrich celebrations and festivals. They can combine their skills and creativity to organize vibrant, culturally rich events that bring the entire community together.

Entrepreneurial Ventures

Both generations have the potential to create successful businesses or support entrepreneurial initiatives. The older generation's business acumen can be paired with the newer generation's fresh perspectives to achieve remarkable results.

Social Impact

Collaborative initiatives aimed at addressing community or social issues, such as education, health, and employment, can yield significant positive outcomes. Working together to find solutions promotes a sense of shared responsibility and accomplishment.

Creating Support Networks Across Both Generations

A sense of community is built on mutual support, understanding, and a shared sense of purpose. Creating support networks that bridge generational divides is a powerful way to strengthen the Indian immigrant community.

Intergenerational Mentorship

Mentorship programs that pair individuals from different generations can be established to promote knowledge sharing and personal growth.

Cultural Exchange Clubs

These clubs can provide opportunities for both generations to share and celebrate their cultural heritage. It can encompass language classes, cooking classes, dance groups, and more.

Community Engagement

Encouraging both generations to participate actively in community initiatives and charitable activities can foster a sense of shared responsibility and give back to society.

Support Groups

Creating support groups that address common issues faced by both generations, such as parenting, career development, or cultural preservation, can offer a strong foundation for mutual support and learning.

Advocacy Coalitions

When it comes to advocating for community issues or engaging with the broader Canadian society, forming advocacy coalitions that involve both generations can amplify the community's voice.

Community Success Stories

To illustrate the potential of collaborative efforts between the earlier and newer generations, let's look at some community success stories. During this visit, I discovered that a few such initiatives have been successfully executed in the past. These endeavors took place in various settings, including community halls, religious institutions, and even healthcare facilities.

Educational Enrichment Programs

A group of older-generation community members collaborated with the younger generation to establish an educational enrichment program. This program provided tutoring, mentoring, and access to resources for students of all ages, enhancing educational outcomes within the community.

Cultural Fusion Festivals

Collaborative cultural festivals were organized to celebrate the Indian community's diversity. Both generations pooled their creative talents to showcase the vibrant traditions and artistic expressions of India. These festivals have become annual highlights, fostering community pride and unity.

Entrepreneurship Initiatives

Younger members eager to start businesses sought advice from older entrepreneurs within the community. The cross-generational collaborations led to successful start-ups and the creation of employment opportunities, thus enriching the community economically.

Advocacy on Immigration Policies

Both generations joined forces to advocate for more inclusive immigration policies that benefited the community. Their collective efforts resulted in meaningful changes in the immigration regulations.

A united community is a community poised for growth, success, and resilience. To build a united front in the Indian immigrant community in Canada, both generations must recognize the strength that lies in their collaboration. By amplifying their collective potential, they can tackle challenges, celebrate their diversity, and thrive in their adopted homeland.

Case Studies and Success Stories

In the quest to bridge the generational divide within the Indian immigrant community in Canada, it is invaluable to turn our gaze toward real-life examples and success stories. These stories illuminate the path forward, providing practical insights and inspiration for the community's journey toward unity. Let us explore a series of case studies highlighting communities and individuals who have successfully navigated this divide. We will delve into the strategies and approaches they employed, drawing valuable lessons that can be applied to similar situations across the community.

Case Study No. 1: Ms Sandeep Johal—Empowering South Asian Women Through Art

Sandeep Johal, known for her evocative art, has emerged as a powerful voice in the realm of contemporary art in Canada. Johal's work not only celebrates the artistic spirit but also brings to the forefront pressing issues concerning women of South Asian origin. On 14 October 2023, Sandeep Johal was part of an exhibition titled *Des Pardes*, which resonated deeply with the South Asian community in Fraser Valley. In a heartfelt Facebook post, Sandeep Johal announced the event:

> *Des Pardes* opens at @thereachgallery on Saturday, 14 October from 12-3 pm!
> I worked with a small but mighty group of South Asian women to create a mural honoring the contributions of South Asian women in the Fraser Valley. I did the final touch-ups today and can't wait for the reveal.
> My dear friend @keeratkaur will also be debuting a new work—*Poetics in Vitality*—in conjunction with the exhibit.
> Hope to see you there!

Des Pardes explores and celebrates the vibrant and diverse South Asian communities of the Fraser Valley. The phrase, which can translate to 'home and abroad' or 'motherland/other land'—embodies the sense of longing for and belonging to an ancestral place that is experienced differently across generations.

Personal accounts, archival documents, photographs, heirlooms, and works of art contributed by members of local South Asian Canadian communities are organized around the themes of migration, faith, family, business and livelihoods, oppression and opposition, and contemporary culture.

Des Pardes highlights the importance of tradition and multigenerational family bonds, the tenacity of individuals and communities in the face of adversity and discrimination, and the significant impact that these communities have had in shaping Abbotsford and the surrounding region.

This exhibition was a testament to Sandeep Johal's dedication to shining a light on the rich tapestry of South Asian women's experiences and contributions. Through her art, she not only celebrates their resilience but fosters a deeper understanding of the challenges they have overcome and the strengths they embody.

Des Pardes was not merely an art exhibition; it was a profound exploration of tradition, multigenerational family bonds, tenacity in the face of adversity, and the significant impact that South

Asian communities have had in shaping Abbotsford and the surrounding region. It was a platform for dialogue, recognition, and for bridging generational divides within these communities. It is particularly important to note that Sandeep's Facebook post mentions 'multigenerational family bonds'.

Johal's involvement in this exhibition was not just an artistic endeavor; it was an act of advocacy. Her art serves as a powerful tool for elevating the voices and stories of South Asian women. By showcasing their contributions and celebrating their resilience, she helps unite generations and forge deeper connections within the community. In doing so, she contributes to the larger goal of bridging generational divides and creating a stronger, more closely-knit Indian immigrant community in Canada. Her art is a testament to the idea that through creativity, shared experiences, and recognition, unity can be achieved.

Case Study No. 2: The Multigenerational Sports Club

One remarkable example of bridging the generational divide within the Indian immigrant community can be found in a sports club in Vancouver. This club caters to a diverse group of individuals, ranging from teenagers to senior citizens. What sets this club apart is its commitment to inclusivity. It serves as a microcosm of the broader community, mirroring its age and cultural diversity.

The club offers a range of sports, ensuring that individuals of all ages can participate. The inclusion of sports like badminton and yoga provides something for everyone. It also organizes cultural celebrations that allow members to share their traditions, thus bridging the generational gap. Events like Diwali and Vaisakhi have become opportunities for mutual learning. Both generations have representation in the club's leadership, ensuring that decisions reflect the needs and aspirations of all members.

The sports club, which also has a work of art made by Sandeep Johal, exemplifies that inclusivity, shared leadership, and a variety of activities can bring different generations together. The community benefits from these interactions by fostering mutual respect and understanding while celebrating its rich cultural diversity. The city funds these projects, and the community can benefit by participating in them.

Case Study No. 3: The Poetry Initiative at Montreal

A gathering known as the Punjabi Kalam Kendra Kavi Durbar, which can be roughly translated as The Punjabi Pen Centre's Poets Assembly, took place in Montreal. This event is a remarkable endeavor aimed at bringing together poets of various age groups within the immigrant community. The October 2023 edition of this assembly witnessed the active participation of Punjabi poets, both young and more mature, who fearlessly expressed their hopes, fears, regrets, pains, and aspirations. In my view, this initiative stands as an excellent means to bridge the gap between these two distinct migrant generations.

I owe my awareness of this event to the Punjabi artist Manjit Singh Chatrik, who kindly shared the information via social media. Chatrik is recognized for selling his artworks at a stall located near the renowned Notre Dame de Montreal in the Old Port area. Incidentally, this church ranks among the top ten most beautiful churches I have had the privilege of visiting, which includes those in France and the UK. Regrettably, during my visit to Old Port in the summer of 2023, Chatrik's art stall was closed, and I missed the opportunity to meet him in person.

While these initial efforts have shown promise, it's clear that we need to introduce more such initiatives to foster a deeper sense of unity within the Indian immigrant community in Canada. Fortunately, the Canadian government has shown a willingness to support and contribute to such endeavors. During my visits to various cities, including Vancouver, Calgary, Edmonton, and smaller towns like Brantford, I've witnessed first-hand how the Indian community benefits from the facilities and support provided by city councils. These facilities not only enhance the community's quality of life but also serve as platforms for intercommunity bonding. City councils are open to constructive proposals aimed at bridging gaps and creating a more inclusive and integrated society. The time is ripe for collaborative efforts that strengthen the bonds between people and promote harmony within the Indian immigrant community and beyond.

As we approach the end of this journey, it's time to gather the pearls of wisdom we've discovered. Additionally, let's take a moment to appreciate the enduring benefits of unity and the rewards of nurturing a common purpose.

I strongly believe that inclusivity is the cornerstone of unity. Communities need to open their arms to the diverse needs and interests of both the older and newer generations. It's about recognizing that our strength lies in our differences, not despite them. Mentorship is a beautiful way to bridge the generational gap. By creating opportunities for learning and mutual respect, we can strengthen our community's bonds.

Addressing practical needs, such as career counseling and legal guidance, can help generations come together. When we cater to the unique needs of each generation, we foster understanding and a shared sense of purpose. We've seen how the celebration of cultural diversity can bring generations closer. Through cultural festivals and interactive workshops, we can join hands and create bonds that last a lifetime.

And finally, we've discovered the power of shared values. By identifying common ground and focusing on what unites us, we can build bridges that bring generations closer.

Practical Steps for Individuals and Communities

So, what's next? How can we turn these lessons into action?

Start with open dialogue. Engage in meaningful conversations with people from all walks of life, no matter their age. Understanding their experiences and perspectives is the first step to unity.

Mentorship and learning opportunities are your ticket to personal growth and stronger community bonds. Consider becoming a mentor or a mentee. Share your wisdom and seek advice from others.

Advocate for the establishment of career counseling centers and legal discourse initiatives within your community. These practical services help address unique needs and bridge generational divides.

Join cultural festivals and workshops in your community that celebrate your heritage. These events offer a chance to share traditions and cultural experiences with generations old and new.

Collaborative initiatives, from community projects to social causes, are the embodiment of unity. By combining your efforts, you can create meaningful change.

The Long-Term Benefits of Unity

Unity isn't just a short-term goal, it's a long-term investment in our community's future. When generations come together, they create a stronger, more harmonious, and closely-knit community. This unity helps us build resilience in the face of challenges, empowers our youth, preserves our rich heritage, strengthens our advocacy, and creates a deep sense of belonging.

As we close the final chapter of this book, we must recognize that this isn't just a conclusion, it's a call to action. The importance of unity and collaboration cannot be overstated, and it's up to each one of us to make it a reality. The stories, strategies, and initiatives we've explored are not just words on a page; they are a rallying call to come together. It's your turn to embrace the lessons shared in this book and become architects of unity within the community.

The generational divide can be bridged with one conversation, one initiative, and one shared experience at a time. You are an agent of change, and your actions can create ripples of unity that extend far beyond the pages of this book.

So, as you read these concluding lines, remember that the power to build a stronger, more harmonious, and closely-knit community, whether in Canada or anywhere else in the world, lies within you. Let's embark on this transformative journey together, united by a common purpose – to create more resilient, vibrant, and interconnected communities. Our collective effort is the key to unlocking the full potential of the Indian immigrant communities in Canada, the UK, Australia, and the United States, celebrating our diverse heritage and leaving a legacy of unity and inclusivity.

Together, we can shape a brighter future for all.

Appendix: Some of the Entry Systems for Canada

This list is for quick reference; however, it is neither exhaustive nor in sync with the latest changes. Since the programs are subject to updates by the Canadian government, it's essential to consult the official IRCC website for the most up-to-date information and guidance. The purpose of this appendix is merely to make the reader comprehend the difficult and meticulous processes and checks and balances for entry into Canada.

The Express Entry system

The Express Entry system is Canada's primary method for managing applications for permanent residence for economic immigrants. It is a points-based system designed to select candidates who are most likely to succeed in the Canadian labor market and contribute to the 'economy. Here's a detailed breakdown of how the Express Entry system works:

Eligibility Criteria:

To be eligible for Express Entry, you must meet the criteria of one of the three federal economic immigration programs:

Federal Skilled Worker Program (FSWP): For skilled workers with foreign work experience.

Federal Skilled Trades Program (FSTP): For skilled tradespeople with work experience.

Canadian Experience Class (CEC): For individuals with Canadian work experience.

Comprehensive Ranking System (CRS)

Eligible candidates are ranked in the Express Entry pool based on a Comprehensive Ranking System (CRS). The CRS assigns points for various factors, such as age, education, work experience, language proficiency (in English and French), and other factors. The maximum CRS score is 1,200.

Express Entry Pool

Qualified candidates create an Express Entry profile online, providing information about their skills, work experience, education, language proficiency, and other relevant details. They are then placed in the Express Entry pool.

Ranking and Draws

The Canadian government conducts regular draws (usually every two weeks) from the Express Entry pool. During these draws, candidates with the highest CRS scores are invited to apply for permanent residence. If you receive an Invitation to Apply (ITA), you have 60 days to submit a complete application.

Provincial Nominee Program (PNP)

Some provinces and territories in Canada have their own PNP streams that are aligned with the Express Entry system. If a province or territory nominates you through a PNP, you will receive additional CRS points, significantly increasing your chances of receiving an ITA.

Invitation to Apply (ITA)

If you receive an ITA, you can submit a complete application for permanent residence through the Express Entry system. You will need to provide supporting documents, including police clearance certificates, medical exams, and proof of funds to support yourself and your family.

Application Processing

After submitting your application, it will be processed by Immigration, Refugees, and Citizenship Canada (IRCC). They will verify your documents, conduct background checks, and assess your eligibility.

Permanent Residence

If your application is approved, you will be issued a Confirmation of Permanent Residence (COPR) and a permanent resident visa (if required). You must travel to Canada before your COPR expires to activate your permanent resident status.

Landing in Canada

Upon arrival in Canada, you will become a permanent resident. You will have certain rights and responsibilities, including access to healthcare, education, and social benefits. After living in Canada for a specific period, you can apply for Canadian citizenship if you meet the eligibility requirements.

It's important to note that the Express Entry system is highly competitive, and having a high CRS score is crucial to receiving an ITA. You can improve your CRS score by enhancing your qualifications, gaining more work experience, improving your language proficiency, and obtaining a provincial nomination, if possible. It's also essential to stay updated on changes to the system, as policies and criteria may evolve over time. More points can be gained by bilinguals who are proficient in both English and French.

Also, with effect from 1 July 2023, the Canadian government modified the system to target specific skills and give priority to workers with those skills. The following news release published on the IRCC (Immigration, Refugee, and Citizenship Canada) website explains the system:

News Release

31 May 2023, Ottawa—With employers eagerly seeking to fill countless vacant positions across the country, immigration

> emerges as a vital piece to solving this puzzle. Recognizing this reality, the Government of Canada is building an immigration system that acts as a catalyst for growth, empowering businesses, helping address their labor needs, and strengthening French communities. When combined, these efforts will ensure Canadians benefit from economic and social prosperity for years to come.
>
> The Honourable Sean Fraser, Minister of Immigration, Refugees and Citizenship, announced today the first-ever launch of category-based selection for Canada's flagship economic immigration management system, Express Entry. Category-based selection will allow Canada to issue invitations to apply to prospective permanent residents with specific skills, training, or language abilities. Further details on the timing of invitations for individual categories and how to apply will be announced in the coming weeks.
>
> This year, category-based selection invitations will focus on candidates who have a strong French language proficiency or work experience in the following fields—
>
> Healthcare
> Science, technology, engineering, and mathematics (STEM) professions
> Trades, such as carpenters, plumbers, and contractors
> Transport
> Agriculture and agri-food

By allowing us to invite more skilled workers in these professions, category-based selection supports Canada's commitment to welcoming in-demand professionals into communities across the country. Additionally, by placing a special focus on Francophone immigration, the Government of Canada is ensuring that French communities can continue to live their life in Canada in the official language of their choice.

Category-based selection will make Express Entry more responsive to Canada's changing economic and labor market needs while building on the high human capital approach that has been a hallmark of Canada's successful economic immigration system. These priorities maintain the focus on bringing in skilled workers with the potential to integrate and contribute to Canada's future.

Student Visa

The process for an international student to seek admission to a Canadian university and obtain a student visa typically involves several steps. Here's a detailed overview.

Choose a Program and University

Research Canadian universities and the programs they offer, then select a program that suits your academic and career goals. Check the admission requirements for the chosen program and university.

Meet Admission Requirements

Ensure you meet the academic and language proficiency requirements for the program. Some universities may require standardized test scores such as the TOEFL or IELTS for English proficiency.

Apply to the University

Complete the university's online application form and pay the application fee, which varies by institution. Prepare and submit all required documents, including transcripts, letters of recommendation, and a statement of purpose. Some universities may require you to provide a study permit (student visa) as part of your application.

Receive a Letter of Acceptance

If your application is successful, the university will send you a Letter of Acceptance (LOA). The LOA is a crucial document required for the student visa application.

Financial Documentation

You'll need to demonstrate your ability to cover your tuition fees, living expenses, and return transportation. Prepare financial documents, such as bank statements, scholarship letters, or affidavits of support.

Apply for a Study Permit (Student Visa)

To study in Canada, you will need a study permit (student visa). Apply for the study permit through the Immigration, Refugees, and Citizenship Canada (IRCC) website or at a Canadian visa application center (VAC) in your country. You may need to provide biometrics (fingerprints and photographs) and attend an interview at the VAC.

Attend a Medical Examination

Some students may be required to undergo a medical examination to ensure they meet Canada's health standards.

Background Check and Police Clearance

You may be asked to provide a police clearance certificate or a background check to demonstrate your good character.

Visa Processing

Wait for your study permit application to be processed. Processing times can vary, so apply well in advance of your intended start date.

Receive Study Permit

If your application is approved, you will receive a Port of Entry (POE) Letter of Introduction and a Temporary Resident Visa (TRV) or an Electronic Travel Authorization (ETA), if applicable. You will need to show these documents to immigration officials when you arrive in Canada.

Arrive in Canada

Travel to Canada before the start of your program. Upon arrival, present your study permit and other relevant documents to

Canadian immigration authorities.

Maintain Your Student Status

While in Canada, ensure you comply with the conditions of your study permit. You must be enrolled in and actively pursuing your studies to maintain your legal status.

It's important to note that the process may vary slightly depending on the university, the specific program, and your home country. Therefore, it's crucial to carefully follow the instructions provided by the university and the Canadian immigration authorities and to begin the application process well in advance of your intended start date. Additionally, policies and requirements may change, and up-to-date information is available on the official websites of the university and the IRCC.

The Provincial Nominee Program (PNP)

The Provincial Nominee Program (PNP) is a Canadian immigration program that allows individual provinces and territories to nominate candidates for permanent residence based on their specific labor market and economic needs. Each province and territory in Canada, except for Quebec, has its own PNP with unique streams and criteria. Here is a general overview of the PNP process.

Choose a Province or Territory

Research the different PNPs and decide which province or territory you want to apply to. Consider factors such as your occupation, skills, work experience, and personal preferences.

Check Eligibility

Review the eligibility criteria for the specific PNP stream you are interested in. Each province or territory has its own set of requirements, including education, work experience, language proficiency, and more.

Submit an Expression of Interest (EOI) or Application

Some provinces use an Expression of Interest system where you express your interest in immigrating to that province. If selected, you may be invited to submit a full application. Others may require you to submit a full application directly to their PNP.

Receive a Nomination Certificate

If your application or EOI is successful, you will receive a Provincial Nomination Certificate from the province or territory. This certificate indicates that that province or territory has nominated you for permanent residence.

Apply for Permanent Residence

With your Provincial Nomination Certificate, you can apply for permanent residence through the federal government's Express Entry system (if applicable) or through a paper-based process, depending on the province's specific rules.

Federal Processing

If you apply through the Express Entry system, you'll need to create an Express Entry profile and indicate that you have a Provincial Nomination Certificate. Your CRS score will be recalculated to include additional points for the nomination. This usually guarantees that you will receive an Invitation to Apply (ITA) in a subsequent Express Entry draw.

Medical and Security Checks

After receiving an ITA, you'll need to undergo medical examinations and provide police clearance certificates to demonstrate that you meet the admissibility requirements.

Permanent Residence Approval

If your application is approved, you will be issued a Confirmation of Permanent Residence (COPR) and a permanent resident visa (if required). You'll need to travel to Canada before your COPR expires to activate your permanent resident status.

Settle in the Province or Territory

Once you become a permanent resident, you are required to settle in the province or territory that nominated you for a specified period, usually around two years. This is a commitment to contribute to that region's economy and community.

Apply for Canadian Citizenship (Optional)

After meeting the residency and other eligibility requirements, you can apply for Canadian citizenship if you wish to become a Canadian citizen.

It's essential to carefully review the specific requirements of the PNP stream you are interested in and follow the instructions provided by the provincial or territorial authorities. Keep in mind that the eligibility criteria, application processes, and intake periods can change, and updated information is available on the official website of the province or territory's PNP.

Labor Market Impact Assessment (LMIA)

Obtaining a Labor Market Impact Assessment (LMIA)-approved job in Canada is a crucial step for foreign workers who want to work temporarily in the country. An LMIA is a document issued by the Canadian government that indicates that there is a genuine labor shortage in Canada, and an employer can hire a foreign worker to fill a specific job position. Here is the process for obtaining an LMIA-approved job in Canada:

Determine Eligibility

Check if you are eligible to work in Canada. Depending on your nationality and the type of job, you may need a work permit.

Identify Job Opportunities

Look for job opportunities in Canada that match your skills and qualifications. You can use job search websites and professional networks or reach out to Canadian employers directly.

Apply for Jobs

Apply for jobs that interest you and for which you meet the qualifications. Follow the employer's application instructions and submit your resume and cover letter.

Employer Applies for an LMIA

If an employer is interested in hiring you, they will need to apply for an LMIA on your behalf. They must demonstrate to the Canadian government that they cannot find a qualified Canadian citizen or permanent resident to fill the position.

Job Offer Letter

Once the LMIA is approved, the employer will provide you with a formal job offer letter. This letter should include details such as your job title, salary, working conditions, and the location of employment.

Apply for a Work Permit

With the LMIA-approved job offer, you can apply for a work permit through Immigration, Refugees, and Citizenship Canada (IRCC). Depending on your country of residence, you may need to apply online or through a Visa Application Center (VAC) in your region.

Provide Supporting Documents

Along with your work permit application, you will need to provide supporting documents, including your LMIA, job offer letter, proof of your qualifications, and other required documents. You may also need to undergo a medical examination and provide police clearance certificates.

Biometrics and Interview (if required)

Some applicants may be required to provide biometrics (fingerprints and photographs) and attend an interview at a Canadian consulate or embassy.

Wait for a Decision

Wait for your work permit application to be processed. Processing times can vary based on your location and the time of year.

Receive Work Permit

If your application is approved, you will receive a work permit that specifies the conditions of your employment, including the employer, location, and duration of work.

Arrival in Canada

Travel to Canada and present your work permit at the port of entry to be admitted into the country.

Start Work

Once in Canada, you can start working for the employer specified in your work permit. It's important to note that LMIA applications can be time-consuming and require employers to meet specific criteria. Additionally, some LMIA-exempt categories exist, such as the International Mobility Program (IMP), where foreign workers do not require an LMIA. To ensure a successful LMIA application and work permit approval, it's essential to carefully follow the instructions provided by the Canadian government and consult the official IRCC website for the most up-to-date information and requirements.

The International Mobility Program (IMP)

The International Mobility Program (IMP) is a Canadian immigration program that allows certain foreign workers to come to Canada without the need for a Labor Market Impact Assessment (LMIA). Unlike the Temporary Foreign Worker Program (TFWP), which requires an LMIA to demonstrate that there are no qualified Canadians or permanent residents available for the job, the IMP is designed to facilitate the entry of foreign workers in specific situations where there is a clear benefit to

Canada. Here are some key aspects of the Canadian International Mobility Program.

Exemption from LMIA

The primary feature of the IMP is that it allows employers to hire foreign workers without the need to obtain an LMIA. This exemption is based on the principle that these workers can benefit Canada economically, socially, or culturally.

Open Work Permits

Under the IMP, some foreign workers may be eligible for open work permits. An open work permit allows the holder to work for any Canadian employer, change jobs without seeking a new work permit, and even work without a specific job offer.

Eligibility Categories

The IMP is divided into several categories, each with specific eligibility criteria. Some of the common categories include:

Spouses and common-law partners of certain skilled workers and international students.

Recent graduates of Canadian institutions.

Participants in international agreements and youth exchange programs.

Various reciprocal agreements and treaties cover workers.

Entrepreneurs and self-employed individuals.

Processing Times

Processing times for IMP work permits can vary depending on the specific category and location of the applicant. In some cases, work permits may be issued more quickly than under other programs.

Spousal Work Permits

One popular category under the IMP is the spousal or common-law partner work permit. Spouses and partners of certain skilled workers and international students may be eligible to work in Canada without restrictions.

Reciprocal Agreements

Canada has agreements with certain countries that facilitate the entry of foreign workers without requiring an LMIA. These agreements can cover a range of professions and industries.

Compliance with Conditions

IMP work permit holders must comply with the conditions of their work permits, including working for the specified employer and adhering to the duration of the work permit. Failure to do so could result in loss of status and potential removal from Canada.

Application Process

The application process for the IMP can vary depending on the specific category. In many cases, both the employer and the worker will need to apply to the Immigration, Refugees, and Citizenship Canada (IRCC). Detailed application instructions and requirements are available on the IRCC website.

It's important to note that the IMP is subject to change, and eligibility criteria may evolve over time. Suppose you are considering working in Canada under the IMP. In that case, it's advisable to consult the official IRCC website or seek legal advice to ensure that you meet the current requirements and understand the specific category that applies to your situation.

Youth Mobility Arrangements and Other Agreements

Canada has entered into various international agreements and reciprocal arrangements with certain countries that facilitate the entry of foreign workers without requiring a Labor Market Impact Assessment (LMIA). These agreements are designed to promote cultural exchange, support economic partnerships, and facilitate the movement of professionals and workers between countries. Here are some examples of countries and programs with which Canada has such arrangements.

International Experience Canada (IEC)

IEC is a program that allows young people (usually between the ages of 18 and 35) from specific countries to travel and work in Canada for temporary periods. These countries include Australia, New Zealand, the United Kingdom, and several others. The IEC program has several categories, such as Working Holiday, Young Professionals, and International Co-op.

Youth Mobility Arrangements

Canada has bilateral agreements with several countries that allow young people to work and travel in each other's countries. These arrangements often include open work permits for participants. Countries with Youth Mobility Arrangements with Canada include France, Germany, Ireland, and South Korea, among others.

North American Free Trade Agreement (NAFTA)/United States-Mexico-Canada Agreement (USMCA)

Professionals from the United States and Mexico can often work in Canada under the terms of these trade agreements without needing an LMIA. This includes professions like engineers, accountants, and management consultants.

Mobility Provisions with Professional Bodies

Some professions have specific arrangements with Canadian regulatory bodies that recognize qualifications and facilitate the entry of foreign professionals. For example, engineers may be eligible under the Engineers Canada Mobility Agreement

Reciprocal Agreements with Individual Countries

Canada has entered into reciprocal agreements with countries that cover specific occupations or industries. These arrangements allow workers from these countries to obtain work permits more easily. For example, the Seasonal Agricultural Worker Program (SAWP) allows agricultural workers from countries like Mexico and Jamaica to work in Canada seasonally without an LMIA.

Global Skills Strategy

While not specific to countries, Canada's Global Skills Strategy aims to attract high-skilled talent from around the world by providing faster work permit processing and exemptions from the LMIA requirement for certain high-skilled workers and researchers.

It's essential to note that the list of countries and agreements may change over time, and the specific eligibility criteria and conditions can vary depending on the program or agreement. Therefore, it's important to check the official website of Immigration, Refugees, and Citizenship Canada (IRCC) for the most up-to-date information and to ensure that you meet the requirements for the specific program or agreement that applies to your situation.

About the Author

Aparjeet Nakai is a seasoned logistician, having dedicated 22 years to the Indian Army, reaching the rank of Colonel. Beyond the military realm, his fervor for exploration has propelled him across the globe, where he has traversed not only diverse terrains spread over five continents but also conquered international marathons, including the Dubai marathon. A polyglot proficient in English, Punjabi, Hindi, and French, Nakai shares his insights on history through his blog, 'Anecdotes of the Ages.'

Passionate about dismantling stereotypes and fostering inclusivity, he actively engages diverse audiences, especially the youth, imparting valuable lessons on overcoming prejudice.

The Brown Goras of Brampton is his first book and a testament to his rich experiences and unwavering commitment to promoting understanding in a world often marked by preconceived notions.